A Fight for My Life

Maryellen Hoffman

PAGE PUBLISHING
Conneaut Lake, PA

First originally published by Page Publishing 2024

ISBN 979-8-89315-252-4 (pbk)
ISBN 979-8-89315-227-2 (digital)

Printed in the United States of America

Heather, for always having my back and supporting me with every decision and encouraging me for every adventure along the way, thank you for always being my chosen family.

Contents

Introduction..vii
Parents' Love Story and Beginning 1
Their First Loss 5
Conceiving..7
My Basic Morals..9
Learning to Live in Fear 11
The Only Girl 15
Brothers 17
Hank...20
The Year It Changed 22
Moving On 25
Losing 29
Growing Friendship 31
Morning at Lizzie's 34
Alabama Summers...38
Undiagnosed Brother 42
Absent Father 44
Sleepovers...46
My First School Bully..52
Chief Rainbow 54
Middle School...56
Last Alabama Summer...58
Return to Connecticut 61
Attention Seeking...62
Overnight Summer Camp 65

Flirtatious Little Sister 67
Fun Club 69
Losing My Brothers 71
Getting into High School 73
Freshman Year 76
Broken Brother 78
Upon My Sixteenth Year 79
Unleash the Crazy 82
Adding Excitement 86
My Arrest 90
Carny 92
Life Change 94
The First Letdown 96
Parenting Classes 98
The Kidnapping 100
The Rape 102
Pregnancy 105
Daughter's Major Trauma 107
One Last Hit 109
Finally Divorced 111
Maybe PCOS 113
Being a Better Momma 114
A Slight Family Gloss 115
LDS Church 117
My POV on Christianity 120
Breaking Point 122
Learning to Have Faith in Myself 124
Learning to Enjoy Sex 127
Reconnecting to the Goddess 130
Facing Trauma 132
Loving My Life as a Single Divorced Mother of Two 135
Falling Fast 136
Letting Go 139

Introduction

I'm never going to remember every good or bad experience in my lifetime. It really does not matter in the end. I am sharing these details and events because I feel there are people in the world who have been through similar situations. I hope to help them find their inner strength to fight for themselves, make the necessary changes, and live their best lives. With all this being said, please remember, there are things that are going to be of a very delicate subject matter and triggering for a lot of people. This is a story written from an adult perspective. I do include content about subjects such as molestation, rape, sexual activities, illegal behavior, and overcoming abuse and neglect. If you are easily triggered, do not read this story.

I have been through more trauma than anyone I have ever met. I am a complete open book. As such, I have shared the basics of my story many times. I was raised by parents who did the best they could, although they did let me down. I forgave the people who harmed me, and I have moved forward in my life. I learned carrying anger and hatred in my heart was too much of a burden for any single person. I had to choose to let that go so I could decide to move forward and live my life without fear taking over. I chose to write this story because I want to inspire others to do the same. I want people to know they are not alone. If I can overcome these horrific events that took over my entire formative years, you can overcome anything you have experienced also.

"The same boiling water that softens the potato hardens the egg" (Russian proverb).

You are not the things that have happened to you. You are not the circumstances you were born into. Finally, you are not the situations you find yourself in. Every single person on this planet is human. We all have faults and make mistakes, and we all aspire to be something better. I consider myself a goddess because inside myself, I have found my inner power to forgive and live my life pure of heart. I am a survivor. I am strong. I am resilient. Among all else, I am who I was born to be, and I hope sharing my story and experiences will help inspire others to find the person they are at their own core. I was not always the courageous person you see me as today. I started my life out being very quiet. I was shy, afraid to make mistakes, and meek.

Even to this day, I will find myself going back to those childlike insecurities from time to time. I will have to reassure myself I am my own hero. I have become my own advocate. I am a goddess. I am a powerful human being. I can do anything I put my mind to. I have come too far in my life to give up now. People count on me to be my best every day even if my best today is not as good as it was yesterday. There will always be days where I would much rather stay in bed crying because my heart is hurting. I may want someone to come take care of me. Yet without all my experiences, good and bad, I would never have become the person I am today. I would never be able to share my story or have the strength to put these words on paper. Most of the names and identifying details have been changed or left out to help keep their identities anonymous. I do not want to affect the lives of the people who do not deserve the pain that would be caused from bringing attention to the monsters in my story.

Every single person is the main character in his/her own story. Each one of us has heroes and villains. I grew up with my teachers asking me "Who is your hero?" and I never had an answer. Now when someone asks that same question, I can answer without a doubt, me. I have become my own hero because without learning how to stand up for myself, I would have repeated the choices I made as a teenager.

I would have continued a cycle of abuse, never understanding why the men I was choosing kept doing the things they did.

I had the opportunity to learn how to use resources. I took advantage of them and used each one to help me slowly climb out of the depths of despair I realized I was in, and I chose to make drastic changes before I found myself making the same mistakes repeatedly.

Parents' Love Story and Beginning

All great people begin somewhere; like many, I'm beginning with my parents. They are an amazing couple, great people who went through some bad times. I won't go into their details because that does not matter in my tale, and it is not my information to share. I will say during their worst, most stress-filled times is when I was hurt the most. I do not blame them for not having time for me. As I said before, they did the best they could with the tools they had available to them. They were raised during a time when emotions were not talked about, and what happened behind closed doors was kept there.

I have always felt it was my responsibility to protect my parents from knowing how I really felt about their failure in protecting me. I love them deeply; they did the best they could and tried. Even though they did not have the knowledge required to keep me safe, I was able to obtain it on my own later in my life. Parents' number one job is to shield their children from every type of danger, and mine did not do that for me. They did what their parents taught them.

Their story is one of love at first sight. My father loves to tell us the story, and we grew up hearing about how he saw her and knew right away that that was the woman he wanted to marry and have a family with. Everyone who knew him thought he had lost his mind. If I had been around then, I would have thought the exact same thing. Who sees someone and makes that kind of life-changing decision without even talking to a person? My dad, that's who!

My father saw my mother and just knew in his heart how he felt about her. He lights up when he talks about how much he hoped and prayed she would go out with him and how he had to get his little brother, James, to have his best friend, Jean, who was dating her best friend, Mary, to set them up. Then they went out, and it was a match made in heaven for him. They spent the next fifty-two years together, fifty-one of them married, until she passed away in front of him. My father loved her every single day. My mother was young, just out of an all-girls school, home to start her new career and life. Every day, she was hanging out with her friends after work, enjoying life as it came because that is what you did in the 1960s. "It was a time of free love," my mother said once. Each day was a party filled with top-down convertible car rides, friends, a little bit of work, and a few protests from time to time.

My father knew right away he wanted to spend the rest of his life with my mother. He saw her, feeling a lightness he had never experienced before. Their first Christmas together, he asked her to marry him. They waited a year so everyone knew that he did not ask her because he had gotten her in trouble. He has always been an honorable man. He tried to keep his future in-laws from thinking anything horrible of their only daughter. My grandparents offered him a lot of money to leave her alone. His heart belonged to her. They made outrageous offers and threats to each of them, trying to convince them that they were not right for each other and they should not spend their lives together. Nothing they could say or do was enough for the two of them to give up their love. They did not want their daughter to be with this working-class man who had basically nothing, causing her to give up every luxury my mother had been accustomed to.

My father was raised by two alcoholic parents. He went to work in tobacco fields when he was twelve just so he could bring home money to help feed his younger brothers and sister. He was accustomed to hard work, providing financially for his family, and never seeing the people he loved the most because he had to work. When he was fresh out of high school, he began working in construction, building houses.

After gaining experience and knowledge, my grandfather and father decided to go into business together. They started a foundation business. This was something the two of them had dreamt about for a while before they finally committed to it. The business was growing when my parents got together, but my mother's parents thought it was going to be a failure.

My mother was the opposite, basically raised with a silver spoon—that is my opinion—until she married my father, making her family become very distant. My mother was raised surrounded by love. Every single day, her family had most of their meals together. Her father was a retired Navy veteran and was now working in factories because he wanted to have pensions for his retirement plan. Her mother took care of the day-to-day housework and kept the two children on a strict routine of school, tutoring, music lessons, and numerous other things she never told me about. My grandmother made sure both kids knew how much they were loved even though my granddaddy had a difficult time voicing his feelings because he was much older and raised during a different time.

My mother spent weekends with her grandparents. They usually did something special and made memories my mother cherished and told me about as I grew up. She had regular tea parties and had dinners on fine china with special silver. There were monthly parties where she wore beautiful dresses, and her brother had to put on a suit so they could dance and mingle with other socialites. These are details I cannot share because some I do not know, and others I think she may have exaggerated.

My father took care of his siblings, sharing a lot of the responsibility from a very early age. He experienced death for the first time when he was a small child. His baby brother died—from what I can make of his story, it was SIDS—during a nap while their grandmother was watching them. Deaths happened so often he became numb to grief before adolescence and hated to wear any kind of suit. His mother was born thirteenth out of fourteen children; my father was the oldest of his siblings. Raised in a house overfilled with grandparents, parents, siblings, aunts, uncles, and cousins and no space for anyone to have their own, it amazes me he made it out to be the man I know him to be.

My parents were deeply in love; I never in my life doubted their affection for one another. They dreamed of their lives together. It would be one filled with love, family, and the simple things. They wanted to mix their two worlds. The plan was for my mother to stay home like her mother had done, taking care of the children and house. Meanwhile, my father would work, run the business, and provide everything they needed.

Life had different plans.

Their First Loss

Having children did not come easily. My parents were married in the autumn of August 1972 and began to work on creating their own family right away. Conceiving was not easy when they finally got their wish. With their first child, a little girl, my mother experienced her first real heartbreak. They had painted the nursery and prepared in every way you do when you are excitedly expecting your first child.

Everything was going well until the winter of 1973 when my mother slipped on a patch of ice. She was then put on bed rest and followed every order. Immeasurable changes have happened in the medical field since this time. The medical team never caught on to the fact that during that fall, the placenta had been pulled away from her uterine wall.

My mother carried the baby full-term and delivered a deformed stillborn little child. They were heartbroken, grief-stricken, and lost beyond comprehension. Conception wasn't easy to begin with, but then for her to go through her entire pregnancy, regular appointments, and everything for it all to end abruptly and tragically as it did would crush anyone. It was a pain no one should have to endure, yet too many have in some way.

Fresh in their shared grief, my parents were unable to come to a compromise. My father did not want to name her. Having experienced death so many times in his life, he wanted to forget this past year filled with joy and excitement that had been crushed in an instant. My mother, afraid of losing him and who never had experienced a pain or grief like this, followed his wishes, unable to voice her own desires of naming her. My mother named the baby in her heart and kept the number assigned to the child. She always remembered the burial location, an unmarked grave next to the small brick Catholic church they were members of at the time. Each time we drove by that place, my mother would point out where Donna-Lou was buried. Every year, I would know her birthday, May 20, 1973. I was told I may be my sister reincarnated. I think it was the only way my mother was able to cope with her grief. She had demons to carry. I believe everyone has them, and we all have to figure out how to carry on so we may live our best lives.

Conceiving

____

After years of fertility treatments, they finally had my oldest brother, Sebastian, the golden child. Three years later, they had their second, my brother Stephen, and finally, their precious little girl. They had numerous miscarriages throughout the years, including another miscarriage with another boy when I was about eighteen months old. They had planned to name him Skylar. In the end, they were comfortable with their sixteen-acre, four-bedroom house in a small Connecticut town, a successfully growing construction business, and a loving family.

My mother was living the best life she could carrying the grief she had never known before the numerous miscarriages and loss of now two babies. She did the best she could to be happy and provide the best life for the three children she did bring into the world, resenting herself for being unable to give my father more children. Every morning, she woke early to make breakfast for everyone and lunch for my father to bring to work. She was a teacher's helper in the classroom and a den mother at Boy Scouts for both of my brothers, dragging me along to every scout meeting and event. I was an unofficial Boy Scout until my brothers decided they no longer wanted to be in scouts, and it was my turn to be a Girl Scout, but I didn't like the girls' version.

The house was kept spotless, a thousand-piece puzzle always sitting on a table in the front room waiting to be worked on, on which I was allowed to put just a few pieces at a time. Colorful jars of dried fruit were cut up into tiny pieces and aligned on the back wall of one counter in the kitchen.

My mother baked; she taught baking classes and sewing classes to make extra money. She sold countless clothing items to other mothers and blankets at craft fairs. I was the little girl she always wanted, and she taught me every one of her creative skills. I have always been an artistic child, the only one of the three of us who showed any creative talents. My mother fed into those and let them develop as much as I wanted to. Stevie did not like that our mother was spending most of her time with me. He also had no problem letting everyone know he felt I was her favorite.

Sundays were for church and family time. During the week, my father was working before I awoke. We had school or preschool, chorus practice, and scouts. Saturdays changed depending on the weather. Sometimes, I was at my grandparents' for the day, or my brothers were there the entire weekend, and sometimes, I was home. Every single night, we ate dinner together.

Since both of my parents were raised in the Catholic church, Sebastian went to a Catholic school. My family followed the traditions they were accustomed to. Something had happened when he was in elementary school that had caused them to take him out of the private school and put him in the public school. My parents switched churches and religious practices due to the situation. Everything happened before I was old enough to understand or remember what was going on. I was baptized in the Catholic church. I don't remember Sebastian ever wearing the signature blue pants, dress shirt, and tie I recognized as I got older from other children who went to that school.

My Basic Morals

Through the years, my parents tried to teach me the most important morals in life. Before bed, they read me a children's bible. I asked questions that they did not know the answers to, doing their best to give me some understanding as they saw it. Sometimes, I took their lessons a bit too seriously. I am honest to a fault. I grew up hating all types of alcohol and drugs because it would cause the person consuming it to turn into a monster. I thought most exaggerated stories had happened exactly as they were told.

My uncle James had died the year before Stevie was born. My mother was pregnant. He went to his friend Jean's house, and they had hidden the keys before they started drinking. Around 2:00 a.m., he found the keys to his car and wanted to go home. After searching nonstop, he discovered the hiding place. He drove drunk, going the wrong direction, turning onto a major highway with his headlights off and into the direct path of an oncoming eighteen-wheeler that had no clue he was coming at him. This had me living in constant fear of alcohol, driving in the dark, and disappointing my parents.

My father had a lot of patience. When he lost his temper, he was the scariest man on the planet. I remember hearing him screaming at Stevie, "I could kill you!" I did not know what happened. I heard the hitting, the screaming, the fear in my brother's cries, and the anger and a tone to my father's voice I never wanted to experience myself. I was committed to making sure I did anything he asked me to do or not to do. I tried everything possible to follow his instructions to the best of my little abilities.

As an adult, my father told me about the event he blamed for scaring his youngest two children. Stevie had gotten into his shotgun shells and took one apart; pellets were spilled everywhere. When my father came in, he was reacting in shock, terror, and fear. He blamed himself for causing a lot of Stevie's issues. He believed that one phrase was taken too seriously and out of context, that as children, we did not understand he would never purposely harm us and wanted to protect us the best he could.

My father told me when he was younger, his temper was hard to manage. He would react without thinking. He got into drunken rages with his own father until one day, they got carried away and decided that was the last of them getting each other's goats. They were no longer going to roughhouse with each other. When they started drinking, the lines of what was fun and serious became blurred. I never knew my father was the kind of man he was trying to protect me from.

When my parents finally had Sebastian, they had a hard time figuring out how to be good parents. My father repeated things that his own parents had done. Thinking it was for the best, he pulled away from being there as much as he should have been. My mother did not have the same option as the main care fell to her.

Learning to Live in Fear

Upon packing for a trip to visit my grandparents down south, Sebastian was doing what any eighteen-month-old would do to help. He climbed into the suitcase and unpacked the freshly folded clothes, throwing them askew. My mother turned her back to find the bed was covered in the items she had just finished packing and began to hit her son. My father ran into the bedroom with rage, grabbed hold of her arm, and stopped her. He scolded my mother, telling her she would never lay a hand on his child in anger again. When he was around, she never did.

The thing is, when you're a person raised in trauma and you repeat the things you're taught, you never really learn how to change those lessons. You have to go out of your comfort zone. You have to choose to learn new techniques to protect the next generation. You have to be willing to let go of everything you are in hopes that one day, you will be better than you were before you entrusted yourself to something you had no idea if it would be better than what you grew up knowing as normal.

My father was raised being hit, protecting his younger siblings and cousins from being hit. He was going to protect his children. My mother was occasionally hit for misbehaving. I don't believe there was a warning as when she reacted with me, there was never a warning beforehand.

There were horrific, traumatic moments sprinkled throughout my childhood. Most of the time, I was witnessing yelling, which was usually the worst of my father's temper when he was with Sebastian. There was one occasion when he got really angry with me. Neither of us remembers what I did to make him so upset. We agreed it was something childish, and he had overreacted at the moment. I ran into my bedroom, slammed my door, and locked it, fearing my father because I knew that look. This was the look I usually received from Stevie right before he threw his hand around my neck, picking me up and choking me because he was angry. My father was a lot bigger than my brother.

I was screaming in fear; my father was yelling in anger. He wanted me to open the door so he could spank me or something. I, of course, refused to let him hit me. My mother had done that enough; I did not want him to have a chance. He kicked my closed door in frustration, broke through the hollow wood with his bare foot, and broke his toenail in the process. I remember hearing him cursing. Then everything calmed down. I stayed in my room for a long time after.

Unsure of what to expect, I kept the door locked. It had protected me just as he had intended the door to do. My father never expected I would be using the locked door to protect myself from him as it was usually Stevie or my mother who was looking to hit me.

My father only ever flipped out on me twice in my life. The rest of the time, he tried to protect me. At the time with the door, I was preteen and hormonal. I likely did or said something that would have made any father flip out. The only other time I had done something was long before that; I thought I could outrun my father. I said something to him that I knew was a trigger to get him angry and ran as fast as I could. My long hair was my enemy that day. He grabbed my ponytail and pulled me back. He heard something and let go instantly, frozen in shock.

I looked up at him with childlike eyes. "What?"

He paused, and my crying stopped. He thought he had pulled my hair off my scalp. My mother had spent so many years desensitizing me from my hair being pulled that it didn't bother me anywhere near like he thought it had.

I do not remember what I was upset about, but he was in the midst of taking care of getting a chicken ready for dinner. I was really upset about it. He had the bird by its feet, unconscious, about to behead it. I said something really mean to him. Knowing how I was at the time, I assume I probably said he was committing murder. Forget the fact that we had a chicken farm and this was a regular occurrence. I quickly learned that chickens did not just arrive at the grocery store, and the reason the chicken at our house tasted so much better than my friends' was because we did not get it from the store. At least they let me miss out on the really gross parts. Somewhere around that time, they made rabbit stew, telling me what we had after I tasted it. I thought it was different and could not figure out why. I immediately got violently ill. Then I became a pescatarian for months, refusing to trust them with my dinner plate.

My father's temper could flip in an instant, though he never flipped out at me like he did on my brothers—until the door situation. I think that day was the day he realized that he had a problem with his temper. Maybe it was just a bad day for him, and I had said the right thing to set him off. It could have been the perfect storm brewing, and the pressure of everything had just exploded. Luckily, no one was seriously hurt that day. My father and I can look back and laugh at the broken door because we both talked about what had happened. He and I are a lot alike; we are overthinkers. We like to address issues if we know we have them, and we are brutally honest whenever we can be.

Although my father was rarely around for most of my childhood, when he was there, we had memorable moments. He protected me the best he could.

My father believed kids were kids and they could do no wrong. When they were fighting, it was sibling rivalry because he had siblings, and they all fought over things and got over it. My older brothers almost always lied about whatever they were doing; he usually assumed I was doing the same. He never realized I had witnessed his flip-outs to my brothers' misbehavior when they lied to him, reacting before he thought.

Sebastian was working on a car in the driveway. I do not know any of the details. There was a dent in the side of the car. My father asked him about it. Sebastian answered, "It was the jack."

My father slapped him and began yelling in his loud, deep, grizzly voice, "How could it be the jack? Gravity would have made it hit the ground! Do you think I'm stupid?"

I remember fear taking hold of me again. I was never going to lie to my father. I would much rather disappoint him than for him to catch me lying.

Sebastian kept doing things that made my father angry, becoming a monster. I remember every single time he did something, I would try to make a note as to what caused it. Then I would do my best to prevent myself from following the same fate.

The Only Girl

I was the princess, afraid to mess up, afraid to break rules, and always quiet. I played outside alone with our pup, a miniature collie, barking at me whenever I began to leave the designated areas. I would climb into the rabbit cages to snuggle the Flemish giants my father won blue ribbons for. According to everyone I asked, I never did anything too mischievous. I threw weeds into the chicken coop because the girls loved the weeds, and my father had no problem with me feeding them "water weeds" as I called them. I always knew the basic rules; I pushed boundaries very little, never really crossing any until later in life when I started hanging out with the wrong kind of people. At that point, I am lucky I did not end up having a fate much worse.

I would go into the rabbit hutch, a building my father built, and climb into this particular rabbit cage. It was as big as a large dog kennel; the base was reinforced so I would not fall through. This rabbit must have been mine. I would climb in regularly. She would snuggle into my arms like she was a cat. I lay in that cage with her for long periods, petting her soft brown fur, running my tiny fingers up her gigantic ears, talking to her. I remember climbing the few small bales of hay my father stacked to make stairs so I could easily enter the cage and the sweet, pungent smell as everything lingered in the air. The rabbits did not smell like the chickens or any other farm animals. Rabbits are clean. They prefer to use the same place for their toilet. I climbed into the wire cage, crawling into my place in the hay next to her.

My father was never upset when he discovered me in the cage with the rabbit who loved my attention, just that I had gone outside and failed to tell anyone when I was sneaking off. I do not remember if I ever gave her a name. All the rabbits had a number tattooed on their ears. Each number had something to do with their breeding and the records. My parents kept detailed notes of each rabbit. The ones who won ribbons had them hanging outside their cages.

*****

My father's father was my favorite grandparent when I was really young. He was the only grandparent I had any kind of special relationship with. I spent a lot of time at my grandparents' house, and he always made sure to let me know I was special. Grandpa kept a cutting board with a knife and cut up cheese, pepperoni, and crackers sitting on the coffee table in front of their couch every single day. I would go over and sneak it while he was sleeping.

If I put my hand near the knife, he would grunt at me. Looking back, I guess he was never really asleep. He let me think he was. He called me his princess. I was the only granddaughter out of the grandchildren. I knew I was treated differently. I still loved doing whatever the boys were doing. I never saw a difference between us. Our gender did not matter; we had to love ourselves.

Brothers

———————

I believe every big brother has a special trait built into them that says they have to torture their little sister. Also, they are supposed to protect her from their friends. They are allowed to hurt her but no one else. I will never understand that logic, and I am proud to say my own children do not abide by the same rules. Stevie was what I call *the special child*. He always needed a little extra attention. He was caught taking a candy bar from the store. I ratted him out; I got in trouble too.

Later, when he took a book of matches, I didn't say anything for my own preservation. I was going on three, and he had already turned six. I felt he knew a lot more than I did, and if I did not listen to him, something awful would happen.

We got home from grocery shopping. Like any other day, our mother put us in our shared bedroom for a nap. After a while, Stevie woke me, telling me to come over to his bottom bunk. He wanted to show me something really cool with the matches. I remember lying across the comforter and pillows. The fabric felt scratchy instead of something soft like I use today. The pillows were thin and worn out.

Stevie began with striking a cardboard match on the backside of the book; it hissed as it lit. There was a smell of burning sulfur as a tiny flame came to life. He'd shake it a tiny bit and drop it. As he kept going one match at a time, this little black "Finest" paper matchbook getting smaller and flimsier, his confidence kept growing, and he began to shake each match less and less as he wanted to see how long it would take for the flame to go out on its own falling from the bed to the floor. Eventually, one of those matches never did go out. It hit a few pieces of paper or something under the edge of the bed, and flames grew.

We jumped out of the bed. He grabbed a tiny toy bucket to try to put the fire out, and I ran to get Mom. She was sitting in the kitchen in her usual place, talking to my grandmother in Alabama. I told her there was a fire. The event became a blur as the flames grew larger and larger. There was a smell of everything burning, and my body was frozen in fear.

My father said she grabbed the dish tub of water and tossed it onto the fire, but it had oils from the dishes likely fueling the flames. My mother had Robby run outside to our safe tree and wanted me to go with him, but I was too afraid to leave her. She had to carry me outside because I refused to let go of her. Everything went up in minutes. My mother spent my life telling me it was my fault that our house burned to the ground because I wouldn't let her get the fire extinguisher from her bedroom. I was too small to know anything more than it was really scary and she was my mother. I probably saved her life because if she hadn't come out with me, she could have died trying to save the house.

For Christmas that year, I wanted a doll, a particular doll. I do not remember what she was or what made her special. My parents and grandparents could not find it after it was destroyed in the fire. Everyone had tried; everything was lost that first December week. My father felt humbled by the experience. He was not upset about losing everything. Tragedies happened. He had homeowner's insurance, which covered everything material. Most importantly, his family was safe.

After the fire, we spent time in a hotel, then lived in a trailer in the front yard as they rebuilt the house, changing the floor plan from what was originally decided upon. My gram came for a while and stayed with us, sleeping in my new princess bed in a pink room with a white canopy bed. I was living the dream of a little princess, tea parties with my gram and great-aunts. My great-grandmother slept in my bed because I kept having night terrors after the fire. I would wake up screaming, afraid that I was going to be burnt alive. She would coddle me and calm me down again. Eventually, the dreams happened less and less. Gram was then able to move with my grandparents in Alabama to their campground.

Hank

———————

After the fire and after my great-grandmother moved south to help my mother's parents, my father befriended a man who was married to my mother's best friend, her maid of honor, thinking he was following what God would want him to do by giving him a place to park his trailer. The intent was for this man to have an opportunity to get his life back on track. Unbeknownst to my father, this man was not a good man. He was taking advantage of my father's generosity, teaching my brothers to devalue women and many other horrible things.

When my father discovered this man was hitting his wife and doing other things, he told the man to leave his property. The man did what any abuser does; he cycled around. He waited for the dust to settle and came back to cause his wife pain again. This is another group of events that spread across a long period; I don't know or remember.

I have a recurring dream of being at their apartment, taking a nap. Someone, either my mother's friend or Stevie, was telling me to hide in the closet or under the bed because this scary man was there. He was not allowed to be there. I snuck out while yelling was happening and things were being thrown around. I think I picked up their yellow rotary phone and dialed.

The next thing I knew, a large group of armed officers were surrounding the building. Someone came and got me out through a window. I was covered in a blanket and handed to my father. When

I asked about that day—it did not matter whom I asked—it never happened. That man ended up in jail for beating his wife half to death. He served many years, and I was told I was never there.

The Year It Changed

I consider the year 1990 to be the year everything changed for us, although it was probably not the official year. There were other things that led up to it, and I am sure the events I have dedicated to this year were spread across a much longer span. I am sure the events surrounding what happened with Hank, my brothers, my parents, and his now ex-wife all have something to do with the majority of the stress that caused my parents to lose focus on their true responsibilities as parents. I was merely six years old on Halloween that year, so I am going to keep it as my point of view. The time was a blur; everything was very fuzzy.

My parents and grandparents were very stressed about everything all the time. I spent a lot of time in the back seat of my parents' car, lying across the bench, pretending to sleep as I sang quietly with the radio, watching the stars in the night sky. My parents were talking about whatever was happening, and I wasn't allowed to listen.

My grandparents were both heavy smokers and diagnosed with lung cancer. My grandmother's was more severe than my grandpa's; she had a piece of her lung removed and recovered. My grandpa went through treatments and got really sick. He stayed in the hospital and just kept getting worse. They found his illness much earlier than they found my grandmother's, and they told my family that he was more likely to survive than my grandmother.

The doctors were wrong. That happens; they're human and are prone to making mistakes and bad calls. They didn't know that the type of cancer he had was more aggressive and needed a different treatment than they had been giving him. It was my grandpa's time. I remember being in the hospital and him telling me that no matter what, I was to go trick-or-treating, that it was my job to bring joy to the world no matter how difficult life got, how dark things became. I was the one who had to find the light and bring it out again.

My grandpa told this little tiny girl she had a light inside her that brought a sparkle to everyone she met and it was her job to share it. "Make the world glow." I did not understand those words at the time. I held them close to my heart. I know I am special; everyone is. We all have something we can contribute to make the world a better place. Sharing my story and experiences is my interpretation of his request.

While Grandpa was sick in the hospital, my father had picked up odd jobs. He was not just building foundations anymore. He was also helping his brother and friends to build houses. On this day, they were raising a wall for a new house. The skies were clear. The wind picked up. The group of about a dozen men lost control of the wall, and it began to fall.

Everyone went running except for my father and one other man, who was about half the size of my dad. My father did not want to see the young man be crushed and felt that if the wall crushed him, at least he would have saved the life of another person. He shattered his ankle and ended up with three pins and two overextended knees that never got treated. The other man had no major injuries and was able to go home to his expecting wife.

My mother started working again, the first time since she became a mother. She got a job with her friend, Tina, at a restaurant. My father was tied up with a broken ankle and was doing the best he could taking care of us. The three of us tested his parenting abilities.

Our father was not used to our routines. He did not know what we did when we wanted to get away with extra television time. When we started fighting, he did not know when we were really fighting or if we were just bickering over something.

Sometimes, we were fighting over the television remote. My mother probably would have taken the television away from both of us, sending us to bed early. My father let us duke it out; it ended in a physical altercation. I went crying to him about how Stevie bit my arm. My father told me I should have just let him choose what we were watching.

The stress my parents experienced kept growing; we felt it as children. The fighting kept getting worse. Suddenly, Stevie was picking fights over nothing, getting more violent each time. As the fights continued, my father's response became closer to something like "Stop exaggerating" and "He's not trying to kill you."

Moving On

Time passed, and his ankle got better. My father was able to go back to work. My mother kept working. Getting on the school bus had fallen on Sebastian in the morning, and I would go to my friend Lizzie's house most days after school.

I must have been in kindergarten; everything was completely new and exciting. I always loved when I got to go on an adventure. I had never gone to a friend's house before, and this was my very first time going to anyone's house that did not belong to my grandparents, great-aunt, or some rich cousin in Alabama.

We got off the school bus at Lizzie's stop and met her sister. The house was not visible from the road, and I had no idea where we were going. I was unsure as I followed my bouncing friend to a place she knew so well, trusting her with all of my being. As we continued up the dirt driveway, old stone walls on each side, we came to a large single-family house. From the front, it looked like any normal single-story house I had ever seen, similar to my own boring house but in a different color. They had a wraparound porch put on, and the back of the house looked like it went on forever. I remember thinking I wanted to see how big their house really was because I had never seen anything like it. Lizzie introduced me to her sister, Charlotte, who must have been about twenty and was preoccupied with her group of friends. Charlotte asked if Lizzie and I were all set and could handle getting our snacks and staying out of trouble. Lizzie assured her we were fine and began to show me around the house.

The front door opened into an entryway attached to a giant kitchen with an island, dark wooden cabinets, and really shiny floors. Lizzie showed me where to toss my bag and shoes so she could show me around. There was a front room that was even larger than the kitchen, one wall with only windows, two pianos, a drum set, and a bunch of other instruments I didn't recognize. "This room is where I practice my piano, and you can sit on that couch when I do." There was a small golden-yellow couch sitting against the wall with a bookcase to its left and walls covered in photos.

I wanted to walk into the room. Lizzie put her hand on my arm. "Come here—there's more," she said in her cheery voice as she led me to another room. We walked down a short hallway to the bathroom next because she wanted to make sure I knew where it was, pointing out the door to the basement and one of her brothers' bedrooms along the way, noting a lock to keep everyone out.

"He's a teenager. I don't know—most of the bedrooms have one." I remember thinking that was odd as I followed her, keeping my thoughts to myself.

We took a right into the bathroom, and there was a delicately hand-sewn needlepoint hanging over the toilet: "If you tinkle when you sprinkle, be a sweetie and wipe the seatie." It was completely tacky, and it stuck with me. Lizzie told me her mother made it because she was getting annoyed at the boys for making a mess every time they used the bathroom. There were two sinks along the opposite wall, a huge mirror with a ton of lights, and a white counter. I had only seen a place like this when I was in Alabama, and we went to my rich cousin's house for the annual parties.

Lizzie's family did not seem to have this kind of money. Her mother was a waitress and single. Lizzy pointed out the cabinet for their towels across from their ugly green bathtub that she laughed about not fitting in with the rest of the house. It really did not, and they kept the curtain closed because their mother hated to be reminded of how ugly it was. I never minded; this place was so much nicer than my house. There was always someone around. My own house was lonesome, angry, or empty.

Going through the other door, it opened into her favorite room of the house. "This is the playroom." I would have called it the living room; it had two couches and was a more normal size of a room. There was a hallway leading to more doors, but she said we weren't allowed down that way because that went to the other siblings' rooms. She didn't really have a bedroom right now because they had just moved, and she slept in her mother's room. I didn't think much of it because everyone has their own thing. There were cabinets filled with every kind of toy and game you could imagine, and we played for hours with dolls or whatever we wanted. When Lizzie realized the time, she had to go practice her piano, leaving me to play for a few minutes on my own.

I took that as an opportunity to look around at all the photos on the walls. I couldn't stop noticing them, and I really wanted to ask about each and every one of them. It was my first time there, so I did not. I walked down the hallway I was not allowed to, looking at the things hanging on the walls.

Hanging at the end of the hall was a very large representation of Jesus. There was a crown of thorns, nails in his wrists instead of his hands, and a nail going through his legs where the ankles touched. Tears fell down the face of this emaciated man, and a ragged, dirty cloth covered his privates. I looked at it for a long time, wanting to cry, seeing and feeling the pain he must have felt, trying to understand why anyone would do that. I had already been going to church for a long time, and I knew the story. The background had clouds with very little sunlight beaming behind, and it was mostly dark and gloomy. I could understand why Lizzie didn't want me to go down the hallway; this picture must have really creeped her out.

As my fascination began to run dry, I heard Lizzie calling for me in the back of my mind, pulling me out of my daydream of the imagined pain. I came back down the dark hallway, and she asked me what I was doing. "Oh, nothing. I just wanted to look at the pictures." That's when Lizzie started to tell me about everyone all over the walls, and I got to ask about everything that was in the open.

In the playroom, there were a ton of pictures; some were of military men and women in uniform. They were her siblings, and they were serving, so she didn't get to see them much. There was a group picture that had a ton of people, and I recognized Lizzie, her mother, and Charlotte right away. The few others were hanging alone on the wall in their individual frames, but there were a lot more. "Those are all of my brothers and sisters."

I looked at her in shock. "Your mom had a lot of kids."

She laughed at me and said, "Well, she did, but she also fostered and adopted a lot of them. My oldest sibling is like twenty-eight, I think, and I have a niece that is the same age as me." She talked about it like this was completely normal as my face distorted as if she were from planet Neptune and had grown two extra heads.

I didn't realize Lizzie had so many brothers and sisters. "Holidays must be really busy, huh?" I was baffled.

"Oh no, not really. Most of them don't come home anymore. They have their own family traditions now. I don't know if I've even met all of them or not. That one there"—Lizzie pointed to one of the pictures of a young man in uniform—"he died in service before I was born."

Then we went on to play with her toys until my mother came to bring me home again.

Losing

Come Halloween, we buried my grandpa. It was the saddest day of the year, probably my entire life to that point. I remembered the promise he had me make. I got home and put on my black princess witch costume with tons of tulle and sparkles. I then began my run around the house, asking everyone to bring me trick-or-treating. It was still light outside when I started to inquire about my yearly ritual. Everyone just kept telling me to go ask another person, and I would. Around and around and around, I would go asking the same four people to take this little six-year-old girl in her sparkly witch costume to get candy from the neighbors, all in tears because that's what Grandpa wanted me to do.

There were tears in my eyes as I repeatedly cried, "Grandpa said I need to go trick-or-treating. He said I have to make you bring me. It's not fair. Grandpa said."

They finally caved in. It may have been the constant badgering or because I finally told them we could go to just the two houses, one to each side of us. There were tears rolling down my face as I was screaming about the promise I made my grandpa we had buried just a few hours earlier. Reluctantly, Sebastian brought me out to two houses and let me get candy. It was the shortest night ever. It also would officially mark the change in my entire life.

That night, I felt the only person who really listened to what I wanted was my father's father. Everyone else had brushed me off, and I had to demand what I wanted in order to get it. I was exhausted from running around and screaming my wants. My tears had run dry. Trick-or-treating felt wrong and dirty. I wasn't having any fun; Grandpa said I would still have fun. I asked to go back home after those two houses, crawled into bed, and cried until I fell asleep.

When I was at home, Sebastian usually let me follow him around while he hung out with his friends because my parents needed a sitter and I couldn't always go to Lizzie's house. I was not allowed to tell anyone if they did anything they were not supposed to be doing because young teenage boys are never innocent. I was pretty good at doing whatever it is they were doing and just avoiding saying anything. If my parents did not ask me, I would not say anything, and then I never had to lie. I never lied to protect anyone; I would not be responsible for their behavior. Some days, we played baseball in the backyard or just ran amuck. I normally kept up with them. As long as the boys were not hanging around girls, I was allowed to tag along.

The regular group of boys only included a pair of brothers, but the larger group consisted of closer to a dozen any given day. These two were like my bonus brothers. We hung out together almost every day. I was the little sister, the pain in the ass, the shadow. The oldest of the brothers was always a better big brother to me than either of my brothers had ever been. I still miss him now.

Growing Friendship

Lizzie would sleep at my house almost every time she came over. She was used to going to friends' houses. I had never had a sleepover before that wasn't at my grandparents'. When she was around, my mother usually made sure the boys were off somewhere else. I do not recall my brothers ever being around on the nights Lizzie was around. I did not think anything of it at the time, but as an adult, it makes so much sense now.

Her house was always more fun than my house because she had the best snacks, the best toys, and her mother allowed us to do pretty much anything we wanted. My house was better for sledding and being stuck in my room. We spent a lot of time in her front room with the stereo blasting, singing, and dancing to whatever nineties music was playing. We went outside and explored the days when the weather was nice. We caught frogs along the creek across the street from her driveway and let them go again just because it was fun to catch them.

*****

One day after months of begging, we got a sleepover at Lizzie's house. I arrived like any other Friday afternoon, but this time, it was a little different because there was a bag waiting for us along with Lizzie's mother when we got to the house. Lizzie and her mother showed me where we would be sleeping, in Tina's bedroom.

The room was filled with strange white glass dolls, and there was a parrot in a cage by the window on a tall hook. The window bent around in a half circle with curtains that reached from the ceiling to the floor. The walls were pink, and the bed made my parents' bed look small. Just like every other bedroom, Tina's door had a lock on it. Unlike the other rooms, this one had multiple locks and a special key that she wore on a necklace. For whatever reason, this was normal around here; bedrooms were locked when the occupant wasn't in it.

Bible quotes were framed on the wall on shelves next to little angel babies covering every surface available. There was another door that did not go to a closet; this was a private bathroom with a night light. Lizzie slept in here so she would not have to be in the rest of the house throughout the night. Everyone has their own form of normal; this was theirs.

We set up our pillows and blankets on the floor next to the area away from the birdcage. After having some time to play, we got ready for bed. We put on our pink-and-purple ruffle dress pajamas and brushed our teeth. Her mother's bathroom was decorated in a maroon color, making us feel like we were really special. This room was more adult than the other bathroom. It reminded me much more of the bathroom I had at home except they didn't have a bathtub in here. She showed me their special toothpaste dispenser that knew exactly how much toothpaste to put on the brush, and we flipped her little pink hourglass. We scrubbed our teeth and made each other laugh as we looked like we had rabies and took a lot more time than we needed to while also making a bit of a mess; her mother would be very angry about it later. We crawled into our little nest and giggled with stories and ideas for the next day of what we would be planning.

Waking up was another adventure. I felt lost again as my friend wasn't next to me. I had never tried to sleep on the floor before, and the constant light made it a struggle. I didn't mind; I didn't complain. After the sun was up, I realized at some point when I was tossing around, Lizzie had climbed into the bed with her mother. I couldn't blame her; the floor was really uncomfortable. I wasn't going to complain because I never complained about anything. I lay there quietly, looking around the room, waiting for Lizzie and her mother to wake up, unsure what I was supposed to do as the guest. I really had to use the bathroom, but would getting up cause them to awaken? I couldn't get up and risk waking one of them. I stayed there looking around at this pink-and-white room covered in Bible quotes and angels, trying to decide what kind of woman Lizzie's mother was to have over a dozen kids and still have Lizzie so much later than the rest; she must really like having children.

Morning at Lizzie's

We finally got to start the morning, which I thought had started much later than I was used to at home. We put on our daytime clothes; apparently, pajamas were not worn outside the bedroom here. Lizzie's house was very different from my house in so many ways. We went into the kitchen, and she climbed up the corner cabinet to reach the cereal bowls from above where we could reach. "Why not just grab a chair?" I asked her, confused. For sure, at my house, I would probably have broken a shelf or gotten hit for that kind of behavior. Lizzie just smiled down at me, setting two bowls onto the counter before getting back down the way she had gotten up with a little hop to the floor as she said, "Oh, they don't care. I can do basically anything I want." I was never allowed to get my own breakfast.

Then she turned the cabinet she had just used to climb a bit to reveal a variety of sugary cereals that I was never allowed to have at my own house. "What kind of cereal do you want?" Lizzie asked as she took out a few boxes of opened cereal and set them onto the counter. "I have Lucky Charms, Cap'n Crunch, and Waffle Crisps. There's others too, but these are open, and I really like to mix them." I couldn't believe that this was a normal routine for her. My mother would go nuts if I had even just one of these.

"I'll have whatever you're having," I responded, sitting at the kitchen island, watching as Lizzie buzzed around her kitchen, knowing exactly where everything she needed would be. I was so fascinated that she could do anything she wanted without fear of anyone coming in at any point in time to tell her she was doing something wrong.

Lizzie placed the two bowls on the island in front of her and grabbed one of the boxes of cereal, pouring in just a little bit. "Is that all you're going to eat?" I asked her as she closed up the box then placed it back into its place inside the cabinet. She looked at me with a little half-smile, the smile I knew meant she was up to something as she grabbed a second box and did the same. Next, she repeated the action with the third box. I reached for one of the bowls.

"No, I'm not done yet," Lizzie remarked as she turned to her silver refrigerator, two doors side by side. I don't remember ever seeing one outside the store. Lizzie had both doors open, and she was grabbing one thing after another. I couldn't make out what she was grabbing as she kept moving around and picking up another item from another cabinet then going to another one. She shuffled a few things around and grabbed something else.

"Are we having milk with our cereal?" I asked, confusion in my voice.

"Yeah, milk and a few other things," Lizzie said, an obvious smile still in her voice as she turned around with ice cream, milk, chocolate syrup, gummy bears, sprinkles, and various candies and nuts in her arms.

"What are you doing?"

"Breakfast sundaes!" We both started giggling as Lizzie added a little bit of each item to the bowls then the tiniest bit of milk.

"This looks gross," I said to her as the bowls were now overflowing with a ton of things.

"*Oh!*" Lizzie paused with a look of surprise on her face as she realized she forgot something. "Do you like whipped cream?"

"Yeah…"

"Well, no sundae is complete without whipped cream!" She ran back to the refrigerator, grabbed the ready whip, shook it, and sprayed a pile onto each bowl until they were about to fall over.

"Oh god!" I remarked, trying to figure out how we were going to eat all this.

"It's okay—it's going to taste really good." Lizzie handed me a spoon. We tapped the ends together, each of us smiling. "Now we eat."

"Breakfast of champions."

Each one looked like a pile of colorful dog puke in a bowl even though it was half-melted ice cream and way too much of the other stuff. The counter was covered with a little bit of everything. Lizzie was not neat when she did things. If this was my house, my mother would kill us; I really hoped her mother was not like mine.

I picked up my spoon and took a huge swallow, hoping that this would not make me sick. Just as the spoon got to my mouth, her mother walked into the room, scolding us for having ice cream for breakfast, and she made us a reasonable breakfast instead.

Lizzie and I spent almost every day together, switching between the two houses. We were growing closer and closer in our friendship. We were becoming more like sisters. Lizzie was the sister I had wished for. We always found something to do. We made our own adventures and kept our secrets as our friendship blossomed into something great.

*****

My mother had started working at a restaurant about twenty minutes away as a waitress full-time. Her sunny disposition was magnetic and helped her bring in huge tips that made up for a lot of the income my father had lost. She picked up as many shifts as possible. With her new employment, I was going to start going to a babysitter, and Robby was somewhere else. When we got older, Robby and I were going to have to figure out how to get ourselves to school without her. We did not do a good job with that; we fought every single day because he would fight with me over everything—if I grabbed the glass he wanted or if I was in the bathroom when he needed it. I could have said "Good morning" in the wrong tone, and he would start fighting with me. I would call her at work, and after school, she would take out her frustrations on me. The thing is, on top of getting beat up by my brother, I was then getting hit by my mother.

If I said anything to my father, he told me to stop doing whatever I was doing to cause them to get angry at me. I was alone. If I started getting upset, I was told to go to my closet and cry, where I stayed and wailed at the top of my lungs, screaming, "Nobody loves me!" as tears poured down my face.

My summers growing up were spent in Alabama. During that time, I got to build amazing relationships with my mother's family, and I ran around the campground they built on the family plot in the 1970s. This was during the same time as the sleepovers at Lizzie's house. During the school year, I was living one life, and during the summer, I was living a completely different one.

Each and every summer had something that made it special in its own way. I spent numerous hours following my granddaddy around helping do maintenance around the campground, feeding the ducks, geese, and catfish pond. He showed me how to roll up white garbage bags for the campers in his special way because it was part of the package when they checked in to make sure they didn't leave a mess behind. I helped hold a bucket to collect the quarters from the washers and dryers as Granddaddy made sure every machine was working perfectly before the campers started their daily use.

I sat in the back of his white pickup truck carrying five-gallon buckets holding the sides so I wouldn't fall out. I helped him fill each bucket with catfish food before he put them into the bed. The ducks and geese followed us down the winding dirt road from their special pen with plants and benches for sitting that made for a relaxing place to sit and relax for campers during the day and doubled as a safe place for the birds to bed down at night.

We would shovel scoops of food across the top of the water, and it would come to life as what must have been hundreds of fish came to the top to feed on the floating bits of food, and the birds joined in to fight and have some themselves. Granddaddy always threw a few scoops over to the grass for the birds before he fed the fish. This was the most amazing sight. The fish would just keep going and going. The water was alive until every single piece of food was gone.

One time, while I was waiting for Granddaddy to feed the fish, I wanted to investigate the side of the lake. I stumbled across the nests of one of the geese. There were a few eggs. I ignored the warning honks and discovered what it was like to really be goosed as it chased me bank to my granddaddy's arms, and he picked me up, laughing and saving me from having more little bites to my backside. I learned the hard way to never ignore a goose's warning to leave their babies or nests alone.

Granddaddy was a navy vet and served at Pearl Harbor. He never talked about his experience, although he had many habits that made him the man I looked up to and admired. He taught me invaluable skills I still carry with me as an adult. Granddaddy gave me the attention I was always seeking when I was in Connecticut. My life in Alabama was the polar opposite of my life in Connecticut. Where I was neglected and ignored in Connecticut, I was treated like the little girl I should have always been treated as.

Granddaddy never let me off the campground with him if I didn't have a Southern accent. I joke about it today because it's amusing: "I am his little Yankee Southerner." As I grew up, I discovered that a day or two of being there would cause me to wake up with a Southern drawl, making me blend in as if I was born and raised there just like my granddaddy. He brought me to run errands to get machine parts, pool chemicals, or food for his animals. Anything that needed to be done, I was by his side whenever possible. I attribute a lot of the person I am today to that man and the experiences he gave me during those summers of my childhood.

There were summers when my mother brought me on day trips when she needed to get away from her mother. They had the typical mother-daughter relationship. It's always complicated—you know you love each other, and you also get under each other's skin really easily and just need to take a break. My mother brought me to places like cotton picking in Montgomery. It was this historical village. I learned that cotton plants are very sharp, and I gained empathy for the people who had to gather cotton without bleeding into their bags because that was not easy.

I brought back a few samples of the cotton plants to show my class, and I had planned to keep it for a memory book to go with pictures that have since been lost. Unfortunately, my teacher took them, and they have since also been lost. I don't know for sure if the teacher decided they were just too cool and kept them or if the teacher threw them away. In the end, my memory is the only thing left of that experience. Many of my experiences are all of what I have.

As the campground princess, I was able to run around and steal peaches from the trees that lined the campground's edge. They were huge and juicy, and I have never tasted or found anything like them. They had that perfect flavor and texture, the juices running down your face no matter how carefully you tried to eat them. Granddaddy always knew we had gone to the neighbor's yard and stole them because we would get back covered in juices all over our faces, hands, and clothes. We just never could resist the snack as we ran and ran around the dirt roads of the RV park and rode our bikes, just being kids.

I guess the worst thing I did as a child was steal peaches from the neighbor's yard even though the owners also happened to be family.

One summer, Granddaddy planted fig trees. I never had a fig before that, and I fell in love with them. Fig Newtons have nothing on a fresh fig. My grandmother made jam with them, and that was the best toast I had ever experienced. It was never as good as the peaches, but it was pretty darn good.

The only time I was not directly under Granddaddy's foot was when he was under his tree whittling. I was allowed to come sit with him, but I had to give him space, sit quietly, and read or just relax. This was the time when his mind was full of thoughts that he couldn't shake. Looking back, I think it was his way to cope with PTSD because you had to make sure he knew you were coming to be near him when you were at least thirty feet away. You had to make a ton of noise and make sure he responded, or you couldn't go over. I think something must have happened that made everyone really cautious. I just knew that there were rules about Granddaddy and his special tree. I was not allowed unless he invited me. Eventually, he did. He taught me about his knives, whittling, and how it calmed him when his mind was in a bad place. I never understood it as a child.

Granddaddy always talked to me as though I was a lot older than I was no matter my age. He never said "I love you," but I knew he loved me. He always showed me and taught me things. Granddaddy made time for me when other adults could not be bothered. He taught me how to grow rose bushes from clippings and how to check the soil to make sure everything was the right acidity and dampness.

Granddaddy's closet and drawers were organized perfectly with all of the same clothes hung and ironed in lines. He showed me how he had at least half a dozen of the same items so he had a signature look and everyone would know and remember him. I have done the same thing in my own way. I normally wear all black and usually very similar in style.

Undiagnosed Brother

As time progressed, things at home changed. Robby kept growing more violent toward me as he got into puberty; anything I did or said could cause him to attack me. I could breathe wrong, and he would fly across the room and hurt me. He began to choke me, grabbing my esophagus. This violence would lead me to develop a natural reaction of his hand touching my neck, and my entire body going limp within seconds as I blacked out. I would awaken again after a few minutes and his manic rage had passed. My parents did not believe that I was afraid of my brother. I felt he really did want to kill me; Stevie hated me. They did not comprehend that he had something wrong inside his head and was going undiagnosed.

The same hair trigger my brother had, my mother and father had exhibited. The only one of the three I was able to figure out how to avoid switching the angry switch on was my father. My mother and brother would be activated at any moment. A look, a word, forgetting to say something, every single day, I was walking a minefield in my life, unsure of the explosion I may encounter.

If one of my brothers touched my mother's sewing machine, I was the only one learning to use it. If something was wrong, I got a belt to my backside. If she could not get to my backside, anything she could reach was getting hit. I could tell her I did not touch the machine; I was at school. Nothing mattered, her rage was explosive, and I was the target. I was always the target. I had to hide the welts and bruises.

Stevie seemed to think my mother's violence toward me was not enough. It was like he had to do things that would cause her to flip on purpose. There was always something that made my parents upset. I was the only one around when my mother discovered an item missing or broken, the rage instantly triggered. I was the only one around.

Absent Father

My father worked all the time while I was growing up; he didn't really make time for me. He bought me things and tried to provide the best he could, a new bike anytime he realized I needed one. I did not complain when my brakes were completely bare or my tread was gone. I just kept riding when my bike had nothing left to give. My older brothers would break their bikes within days. Where I would put so many miles on mine that I was lucky if it lasted more than a year from spring to fall. I always loved the freedom I felt on my bicycle; I needed to escape my reality. When I was not on my bike, I was in the backyard hiking and exploring. What is the use of having sixteen acres if I could not have adventures? My mother, on the other hand, was in charge of taking care of us. She was supposed to keep me safe, make me feel safe. She was supposed to spend time with us and make sure all our daily things were taken care of while my father provided the monetary needs. When I was really small, my mother did a great job. She taught me many crafts and skills I still use today. We went hiking; we spent time together as a family. She made me clothes on her sewing machine that were unique and out of fabrics I picked out. I loved being a part of the process even though when I started school, my classmates started making fun of me for having clothes my mother made instead of name-brand things. I began to resent her for making my clothes, and I began to pull away from my mother because I hated the teasing from the kids my age.

In my early years, until kindergarten or so, my parents were very good at parenting. They took great care of all three of us. My oldest brother was becoming a teenager; he got his first job and needed help to deliver newspapers. He needed more and more attention as teenagers do. My second brother was beginning to show symptoms of his mental health issues, and I was still the little quiet mouse of a good girl they relied on. So when life changed, they never realized how badly they let me down because they were so busy taking care of their first two who needed them far more than I did at the time.

Sleepovers

During one of the early or late summers at Lizzie's house, we picked beetles off rose bushes for her neighbor for a penny a piece. We caught frogs by the creek and ran around doing whatever kids were supposed to do in the 1990s. At my house, we did similar things. We had a lot of fun. Lizzie was probably the only person who did not make me feel horrible when I lost my identity. Lizzie helped me remember who I was at my heart, and she wanted me to remember who I was on the inside instead of worrying about the person everyone saw on the outside. Life was fun during the day.

Overnights were far different. We slept in her mother's bedroom. I never thought anything about the three locks on the door or how the master bedroom had its own private bathroom. It was really nice and always super cool to spend all my time with a girl who actually wanted to spend time with me. When Lizzie was not around, I was alone and ignored, and I hated feeling afraid of being hit or yelled at.

I had been hanging out with Lizzie for a long time. Our mothers were best friends and worked together. One night, her older brother David came in and picked me up from the bed really quietly.

David reached his arms under me, one under my shoulders, one under my knees, pulling me into his chest like I was nothing. The scent of him was comforting and familiar; his strength also had a soft touch. I felt like I belonged against his chest, being carried, and he could bring me anywhere he wanted to. This was a good feeling, one

Lizzie had told me I would get to experience eventually by sleeping at her house.

He carried me out of the bedroom in his arms, and it just felt nice. I liked being held against his chest, feeling his heartbeat against me as I pulled my hand up and placed it against his chest next to my face. I wasn't sure what was going to happen next, and I didn't care because I was going to get attention. I was never someone's priority.

David carried me out in his arms on a regular basis. He had keys to the locks on the door; his mother was clueless. I was the only girl he would carry out besides his own sister because I was the only one who had no idea how wrong this behavior actually was.

For me, this felt pleasurable. I enjoyed being carried out, having someone's undivided attention. Lizzie loved me being there because as long as I slept over, this did not happen to her. Lizzie's own issues were growing fewer and fewer. I never complained as I learned how to separate myself from what I liked and what I felt I had to put up with no matter how it made me feel. I did not know any better; I thought this was normal.

My mother would beat me if I did not eat dinner even if I hated it. I would sit for hours, even fall asleep at the table if I held my own. I had no choice; I had to do what she said. In my head, this was the same thing. I had to do whatever I was told. If I got into a fight with my brother, I was not allowed to complain because it was sibling rivalry; I was exaggerating.

That first time David carried me out of Tina's bedroom, he brought me into his own room. The bedroom had light-blue walls, a twin-sized bunk bed, a recliner, a television sitting atop a dresser, and another bed. I thought it was odd to have three beds in this room. He carried me over to the recliner and rubbed my back, making sure that I felt comfortable. David rubbed my thigh, slowly working his way higher and higher under my nightshirt. He told me that anything we did was our secret. If I told anyone, I would be in trouble and he would have to hurt me.

That was enough to make me afraid. The fear of my father's wrath toward my brother from anyone being taken out on me was crippling. I was going to do anything he wanted me to do. Lizzie told me this was normal and okay. It didn't hurt, and it was our secret, just another secret we would have to keep.

David had a way of making me feel safe and afraid at the same time, safe in his arms and the attention he gave me. He was a junior firefighter, strong in his physical ability. His voice was calming; his words came out with confidence. The things he said were the perfect combination of what I needed to hear to make me believe I needed to listen to him.

"I'm going to show you things that will make you a really good wife one day. Do you want to make your man happy when you grow up?" Of course I did. I had no idea what was happening or what he was talking about. He turned on the television, and a man and woman were naked on the screen. I was shocked and looked away and at him.

"No, it's okay. I'm going to teach this to you. Maybe that's too fast." He paused the film so the television was just for light.

He removed his erect penis from his pants. "Do you know what to do with this?" I shook my head. Of course I knew nothing; I shook my head completely unsure what to do. I wanted to run, but the last thing I wanted to do was to be yelled at or, worse, hit. "Can I show you?"

Hesitantly, I whispered, "Okay." I had no idea what I was supposed to say. Lizzie and I had talked about this; I knew it was going to happen eventually. I just was not sure that I was ever going to be ready. She wanted me to experience everything she had. She said it was not bad and that it was something we would need to know for when we were grown up. That we would never learn it in school, and he was helping us by giving us these lessons.

He moved the film forward to show the woman placing the man's penis into her mouth, and licking it. David wanted me to do the same to his member. "Do you think you can do that?"

I remembered what my friend had said. "I guess so."

He pushed Play on the film, and I did my best to reenact what I saw. After a few moments, he stopped me and grabbed something that appeared to be a broom handle then showed me with his own tongue what he wanted me to do. "You have to start off a little slower than that."

Nights like that repeated numerous times with less and less instruction as I began to understand what he wanted and liked easier. My fear began to diminish as time progressed, as my trust grew. David began rubbing his member against my privates, never penetrating me. After he was finished, he would send me into the bathroom and clean myself up.

The sleepovers at my house became a time for Lizzie and me to spend trying to make sense of the things he was doing with us. We learned about our bodies, what touching those places and each other made us feel. As we began to approach puberty, we began to like the feelings associated with those things. We learned we could feel the same way without him.

Eventually, he wanted to try something new. He wanted me on all fours, and he wanted to see if he could put his finger inside me. He asked me to find this space on my own so I would be more comfortable. I jumped the first time he tried. In my next bath with my regular toys for playing like a regular little girl, I discovered a place I had never known existed before. It felt good when I touched this mysterious spot. I could put my finger inside. I wanted to see how deep it was. Why did he want to put his finger there? I did not understand. I used a Barbie leg in my bath and discovered it felt different when I touched it this way.

The next time I slept at Lizzie's house, I was almost excited to see David. I felt like he loved and cared for me. I was making him proud. After the usual oral activities, he placed me on my hands and knees away from him and tried again. This time, he kept going and he really enjoyed himself. Something was different about this time; I didn't know what it was. I left almost in tears, and I began having dreams about that moment, which haunted me well into adulthood.

This became our new normal routine, which continued for a long time. Lizzie, David, and I had a shared secret. I was never really keeping a secret. Since no one asked me anything about it, I did not say a word. I enjoyed the attention I received from him.

During the last encounter with David, Lizzie and I were asleep on the pullout couch. It was a basic nineties couch that every house had. The metal bars could be felt through the mattress. The pillows always fell through the top of the mattress onto the floor. David lifted the blanket and placed his chilled legs against my backside, waking me as I was asleep facing away from him. He rubbed his member against my curves as I pretended to remain asleep for as long as possible. I think his friends were outside on the deck; I don't remember. He shifted his member to being between my legs and thrusted himself, rubbing his member a little bit more, knowing I was now awake as I was responding as he had taught me, instinctively.

David had me roll over and crawl under the blanket, putting his member into his mouth and doing everything he liked until he wanted me on top of him. As I crawled to his chest, I now realized he had brought an audience. This was new. I was now riding him until his penis was inside me. Once he released himself, he let me go back to sleep and went on to whatever the plan was. One of the people in the group told someone, completely changing everything I knew.

Everything in my life became very dramatic. The relationships I treasured most had ended abruptly, and I wasn't allowed to talk to David or Lizzie. I remember a lot of anger and screaming around a lot of the time, but I don't remember what happened when. I feared that David was going to hold up to his threats.

This abuse went on for about three or four years. There were plenty of hints throughout that time. I was in Sunday school, and I had to know how exactly the Virgin Mary was really a virgin because I could not wrap my head around it, already knowing how babies were made.

The response I received was being put into the older class from the younger class, asking the same question with the teenage group, then being kicked out of Sunday school completely. No one thought a small child asking a question like that was a sign of concern. How could they overlook something that, as an adult, I can see is an obvious sign myself?

In fourth grade, learning about sex education, I already knew everything we needed to know about sex. Again, not a single adult thought this was odd. A child should have no idea how a fully mature penis appears. I was able to draw the fine details of the male anatomy we were only shown cartoon versions of during the presentation.

Once I was able to understand what he had done and what he had stolen from me, my nightmares changed. I was unable to walk near the firehouse. I was afraid of firemen. The people whom you're supposed to call in case of your home being burnt to the ground would not be called by me. I would rather watch my house be destroyed than cross the man who hurt me in ways I couldn't understand until later.

David joined the military and is now a fake small-town hero. Yes, he served our country in Iraq and has saved many people. He is also a monster and a pedophile, and bad things deserve to happen to him. He knows who he is. He has to look at himself in the mirror every single day. I never had the courage to stand up for myself and out him for the abuse he put me through.

My First School Bully

When Sebastian started getting us on the bus each morning, I kept my mouth shut as I experienced bullying the first time. A girl multiple times my size in a higher grade began to stick gum in my hair on the school bus. The first many times, my mother figured I had fallen asleep with gum in my mouth. She was convinced I did this all the time no matter how many times I told her someone did it on the bus. Gwen had a daily habit of tormenting me. The gum was the most memorable.

Eventually, after my mother refused to listen to me, I turned to my brothers. This is where I learned that she had a crush on one of them, but he was not interested in her for whatever reason. I had beautiful long blond hair that went all the way down my back, ending with ringlets. Gwen was a bully, and she did not care who knew it.

One day she took scissors and cut a few inches off the bottom; it was probably about a three-inch chunk, and I cried as I had to get a haircut to even it out, bringing my hair from just above my hips to the middle of my back, losing my curls.

After my brother finally said something, adults got involved. The bus driver tried to separate us, but it did not last long. Gwen chewed up three or four pieces of extra sticky gum and put it into the base of my hair and squashed it while rubbing my hair as much as possible to make it impossible for my mother to remove this time.

I remember my mother putting all types of things into my hair, the smell of peanut butter as she coated the gum, trying to penetrate my hair and separate the two. My mother added oil and used a comb to pick and pick, pulling at my skull as I screamed in pain. The gum was not moving in any way from its mess. My hair was getting more and more entangled as my mother tried everything she could think of. We went into the bathtub, where she tried to use ice cubes and shampoo and conditioner to wash the mess of oils and peanut butter from my scalp.

Nothing moved as the water ran through, and my hair was a knot on the top of my head. I was crying for hours; my mother had lost all hope and began cutting the gum, leaving as much of my hair as possible.

We went to the salon again, and I received the worst possible haircut a little girl could possibly undergo. I got a mullet. If I was a boy in the eighties, it would have been a dream. I was a girl; this was my nightmare. All because her brother was not interested in going out with a girl who was slightly overweight and not one of the prettiest in his class. I am sure there were many other reasons, but that's the only one I could think of at the time.

When I went back to school, my classmates were not shy about letting me know how horrible my hair looked. They did not care how much I hated it and what happened to me leading up to losing my beautiful locks. They just saw that this girl who was usually wearing cute dresses with her pretty ponytails and braids was now wearing clothes from her brother's dresser and had a haircut like the boys. Obviously, she was a boy now because that's how it works when you're a kid. You wake up one day and you're a whole different gender.

I refused to wear a dress ever again; my golden-blond hair grew back a dusty ash blond, and the curls I once loved were now pin straight. Gwen took a lot more than just my hair that day; she took my identity.

Chief Rainbow

During all this, there was an event at the church. They had a group of indigenous people putting on a performance in a room connected to the basement kitchen. My mother and her best friend, Tina, had been working hard to make this event happen. I was running around chasing a group of other kids, playing and just being a kid.

I remember this very tall man, unlike any I had ever seen before. He stood taller than all the other men I had ever seen; his hair was longer than his elbows and in two braids with feathers. Surrounded by the scent of cedar and rawhide, he wore tan clothes made out of deerskin that was far softer than anything my mother made me. His shoes and everything matched perfectly and were obviously handmade. I was in awe when I saw this man. I loved looking at him and trying to understand what made him so much different from the other people at the church—his long black hair or maybe his clothes. I didn't care; he told me wonderful stories, and I really enjoyed spending time with him.

As I was running around, he stopped me to say, "Hey, hun, I need you to listen to me for a moment. You're going to get to a place in your life where everything is going to get really hard. Everything is going to get dark. This is when you need to find the light I see inside of you right now. Hold on to that little sparkle, and never let it go."

I looked at him completely confused. Why was he talking in riddles? What was he talking about?

He laughed, putting his hand on my shoulder, reassuring me. "Go have fun. One day, everything will make sense. Just remember to always find your inner light, and know there's always an end to the darkness."

I don't know if I responded or anything, being a shy child, as I ran off doing whatever I was doing. That single moment stuck with me; through the times I was most scared, I remembered what he had told me. I knew that it would always end, and I would always end up okay when it happened. I learned more and more about Rainbow and his Cherokee tribe; I decided I wanted to be just like him.

Through the years, many things happened as the three worlds rotated like the calendar. My school days would have days of mean girls who had to remind me of my ugly haircut. Everyone had to say something about my brother's hand-me-down clothes, so I must have wanted to be a boy now. I never spoke up for myself. I saw no point in trying anymore.

The people I was supposed to be able to turn to made me feel like my feelings did not matter. They did not believe emotional health was important. They did not realize that the words and actions were making a monumental impact on my life. They never realized that I had no one but myself. I turned to journaling as soon as I learned how. My English teacher said I have an incredible talent for story-telling, and I should stick with it because it would be a huge waste of talent if I gave up on the one thing I had that I loved most for my emotional outlet.

Middle School

The next few years in school were difficult for me. I didn't know what friends were real and which ones were spreading rumors. I was succeeding in home economics class. My English teacher told me I should consider being a writer as an adult because I have a natural gift for storytelling. *Was that a compliment or an insult?* In science class, I got to make a unique model of different liquid densities in a really cool beaker. I felt I had to hide my brains. It would just be another thing the other kids would use to fuel their mean words.

In class, I did my work, got great grades, and really enjoyed being a complete nerd, learning new things and excelling. But outside class and in peer groups, I had to pretend I was just like whoever was at the table with me. There was no way I was going to let them know I could say my alphabet backward or that math was my second language. I kept to myself, and most of them thought I was very friendly and shy.

One of our peers was the female top bully, Jeanette. I don't know what demons she had to live with. She went through every single person and started a fight to show her dominance. I remember she went away for a while and came back in eighth grade with stitches on both wrists. I wanted to feel the pain. I was always numb; I had no emotions. I just wanted to feel something.

When I got home, I went to my kitchen, grabbed the sharpest kitchen knife, and did what she had instructed me to do. I slid the blade up my arm. As I felt the cold, sharp metal glide across the thinnest skin of my inner arm closest to my hand, breaking the skin, small beads of blood arose. I still felt nothing; there was no pain. I stopped because I did not want to die; I just wanted to feel anything. I went back to school the next day; she saw the cut and asked me about it. I only told her, "I was trying to feel" as I looked down at my own arm, barely a mark in comparison to the bandages she had.

Jeanette then told me about her own story, how she wanted to die, how she was fighting for her own life and how bad things were at home. I told her about some of the things I had been through on a daily basis, and we were not friends. We understood each other. I never told her about David, only the violence inside the walls at my house as she told me the violence inside her own.

The summer between elementary school and high school, we were both working in a summer job program. She came into our workplace bathroom, sure I had told everyone about her secret. Jeanette wanted to beat me up for spilling her beans. I grabbed her by the throat and pinned her against the wall, the same way my own brother had done to me hundreds of times. I told her something along the lines of I was not a person to mess with and to leave me and my friends alone, and anything that happened at that point was out of my memory.

I left the bathroom in tears, and she got in trouble. Jeanette had a reputation for being a bully and fight starter. I was a Goody Two-shoes and too shy to do anything to anyone. My persona was always spotless. To this day, I do not think I have anyone who can say honestly that I have done a single thing with anger, hate, or ill intentions in my heart.

I never told the adult in charge that day what had really happened. Jeanette had to go somewhere and did not show up again for months. Some rumors say she got into modeling in Europe; some say she went into a mental hospital. It really does not matter because by the time she returned to our class, she was a lot better with anger management. I was her only friend. I never judged her for being the person she was before she left. She needed friends, and I was an ally.

Last Alabama Summer

During my last summer in Alabama, my gram was frustrated with me because my cousin was doing better in school than I was. His father was a teacher, and his parents gave him attention and love whereas my parents probably didn't care if I was alive. She called me stupid, and I flipped out on her. My grandmother and mother said it was my preteen hormones, and that was basically the end of it. I had to apologize and accept that from her point of view, I was dumb because I did not want to show anyone how intelligent I was and add *nerd* or *geek* to the mix of bullying. They didn't care how torturous my life was at home; they didn't understand. I was a screwup who was supposed to take care of the house and make everything easy on my mother. They wanted me to do everything even though I was already trying to do it all, and I didn't know how.

As much as I felt the love of my granddaddy, I felt a sense of being a burden to everyone else. I was never going to be pretty again. I was never going to be smart enough. I was never going to work hard enough. I was never going to be what everyone wanted or needed me to be. I was lost, hurt, broken, and I couldn't feel safe with anyone. The few friends I had had parents who loved them and made time for them doing things that reinforced how bad my life really was. I still couldn't say anything to anyone. Whom was I going to say it to?

If I told anyone about the junior firefighter, David, and the things he did to me, they would blame me for allowing it to happen. It was my fault, after all; I did allow him to carry me out, and I never said anything even when I felt it wasn't right. My body started to shake in fear as I walked past the firehouse because I was afraid he would hurt me if anyone found out what he was doing to me for years. I didn't tell, but still, someone found out, and now my life was in danger. I lived in fear because I had no idea that he had made a false threat in the beginning. That first night when he brought me to his room and told me how important keeping this secret was, he told me that I would be hurt if anyone found out. Through the years of abuse at his hands, he reinforced that message and made sure I knew the pain I felt would be worse than I could imagine. David may not have known how bad things were at my house and how much pain he would have to cause me for those words to ring true. I did, and I feared more pain than my daily fights could possibly be.

That last summer was the year I was twelve; my breasts had developed that year. I had to get a new bathing suit multiple times and wear a shirt at all times. For the first time, I was uncomfortable with my physical body. My grandparents had started hiring local kids to help out with simple tasks around the campground as the business was growing and they needed the assistance. I had been playing at the pool table like I had done since I could reach standing on the step stool Granddaddy had put next to it, and he taught me about angles. He showed me math was in everything, and math was my language. It was the only thing I could really talk about with anyone and understood completely no matter whom I was with.

I was wearing my normal jean shorts and a tank top, and my hair was in a ponytail holder. This was my signature look. I knew exactly how to get every shot I wanted to, but I also knew how to miss them when I wanted to play like a ditz. My brothers taught me how to win money from the campers, and my grandfather taught me how to win. I walked around the table, making shot after shot, having fun and enjoying a conversation with one of the regulars.

The bells on the door chimed as it opened, letting the occupants know someone was entering or exiting the front of the building. In came a group of five slightly rowdy teenagers. They were only a few years older than me, three boys, and two girls. The girls had similar clothes to me, and I felt simple when I looked at them. I never wore makeup; they had the perfect amount. The boys looked like they belonged on the teen magazine covers; they were really cute and walking my way.

I pretended not to notice as my hands started to shake, and my aim became affected, causing me to miss my shots. The group was giggling, the girls obviously flirting.

"Oh, I guess we can't play. The table is already in use," said one of them.

"That's just the owner's granddaughter. We can ask her to play, or we can have her join us," said one of the girls.

I was still shy; I was not good at talking to people. Even at twelve years old, I had no people skills. They asked politely if they could take over, and I stepped back, allowing them to take over and watched as they took turns playing two-on-two eight ball. Finally, I spoke up. "I play the winner."

And the cute single summer boy volunteered to be my partner. We talked and flirted during the game. Sometime while playing pool, my granddaddy noticed us at the pool table. I never thought anything of it.

That afternoon, Granddaddy had to go into town alone. For the first time, he was running an errand without me. I found out later he went to the boy's house to see his family and had a word with him and his father about me. The summer boy never came near me again even though I remember swimming around the pool and having fun. His female friends would come talk to me and hang out, but the boys kept their distance because of whatever happened. It was like I had some kind of plague.

Return to Connecticut

When I got back to Connecticut that autumn, everything was different. The boys who teased me constantly were suddenly interested in me. The girls were now spreading rumors about my breasts or that I was having sex. The other bullying stopped; apparently, wearing my brother's hand-me-down clothes did not matter as much now that I had large breasts. My friendships had never been anything I worried about; my friends were always there. I had different friend groups, and I migrated from one to another like a little social butterfly. I would check in with one group of friends, go to the next, and so on until I made my rounds with everyone. Some of my friends hated each other, but that was fine. Their differences never had an impact on my feelings, and I did not care why they chose not to be friends as long as they were my friends. Most of them didn't know my history, and I was never going to tell anyone. I was always a golden-hearted person who put their feelings first and wanted to make sure they were in good places.

Attention Seeking

I was starving for the attention I was now lacking from everyone important in my life. I never saw my granddaddy, my father worked all the time, my brothers were always off doing whatever they were doing, and my friends had their own lives with boyfriends. Everyone's lives excluded me. I spent much time riding my bike and making my own adventures, trying to get any kind of attention. I was willing to take negative consequences.

I rode my bike from my house to different stores; I stole teen magazines and enjoyed the thrill as I left the premises and somehow never got caught. My friends had their walls covered in posters of the boy bands, and their parents bought them the magazines. My parents didn't want to give me the time of day; forget giving me a few dollars here and there for a magazine I didn't need. My walls and ceiling were covered, and my parents never questioned how when I wasn't working enough to pay for them. I would get snacks because Robby was constantly eating everything my mother bought, and food was a commodity I was not privy to. I never took anything that was worth over five dollars, and I only did it to see if I could.

The excitement I felt in my gut reminded me of the feelings I had when I was with David, something I knew I should not enjoy. It was something bad. I had to chase that feeling. My stomach churned with excitement; the butterflies twisted as I put my hand on the magazine, knowing what I wanted to do. I debated on the cost of what taking that first item would mean—if I got caught, if I got away with it, what it meant if I made it home and no one noticed. I closed up my backpack with a few magazines inside it, bought a small item at the register, and left like I had nothing to hide. I jumped onto my bicycle and rode home.

The excitement of not knowing if I was being followed that first time made me feel giddy. I kept going until I reached my steps, parked my bike, and walked inside to my room, where I took the magazines apart. Then I began to cover my walls to match the ones my friends had, and I could finally fit in with all of them.

I remember a few times having the store security person follow me. I had to dodge them. I almost got caught a few times, but the chase was so much more fun than anything else I did during that time. Those days were the days I would put whatever I had back on a shelf just in case I did get caught. If I had nothing in my bag, there was no reason to be in trouble, at least for that particular day.

I got a little cocky at some point and went to a smaller store where I decided I wanted to attempt to get something there. I had never stolen from this particular place. I didn't know that they had been on the lookout for a group of girls my age who had been doing what I had been. I got caught for the first time. I was brought over to the police department and said it was my first time. I told my story; it was the truth. It was the first time I had ever been in that store. I heard that other girls had gotten things, and I wanted to see how they did it. I didn't give up names because I didn't actually know for sure whom the rumors were about. I had heard the owner talking to my mother, and I used that information to help me get out of trouble. I left out the history of going to other stores because they never asked me if I had ever done something similar anywhere else. I'm sure my mother would have really flipped out if she knew the whole truth.

My mother taught me not to lie, but giving an honest perspective was quite reasonable if it wasn't hurting anybody. In this case, I was getting myself out of trouble, and I was not going to cause my parents any more hurt than I already had. She told me omitting information was not the same thing as lying.

I was released with a warning to never do it again. The owner figured I was a good kid. My parents were good parents, and since

I was so open about my reasoning behind taking things, he didn't want to press charges. That was the one and only time I had ever been caught. I may or may not have tried to chase the thrill since; the world may never know.

Overnight Summer Camp

The following summer, I went to summer camp for the first time, and my Alabama summers were completely over.

My first summer not going to Alabama, I went to summer camp for the entire summer. I was not spending any time with any of my family or my friends. I was going to be completely alone for the first time in my life. I had a stack of envelopes, stamps, and paper to write home whenever I wanted. I had a journal and access to the camp store to buy a new pencil or pen and notebook as needed because writing had always been an outlet for me. I was a timid young girl with no friends, and I was completely alone. The person I felt I was in Connecticut was definitely not the person I was all summer long in Alabama. I cried because I didn't get to go south. I cried because I couldn't be at home. I cried because I was alone for the first time.

I stopped eating when the bullying changed. I was eating one meal a day if you could call it that. I barely ate anything. I wanted to feel good in my skin. I hated that I had gained weight and it all went into my chest and butt. I hated that everyone looked at me differently, and I was now treated like something Lizzie's brother had treated me as. It was an icky feeling, and I didn't want it. I loved flirting, but I didn't want to be sexualized. I wanted to be in control of who got to see me and who didn't.

A few weeks into it, I finally felt good about being at summer camp, making the best of it. Finally, I had a few friendships and was enjoying my days and writing until I was ready to pass out each night. I met Celeste. She was my best friend, and we were mortal ene-mies. We hated each other because no one can have more than one best friend. We didn't know a thing about each other, and the things our shared friend told us about the other person was horrible. We ended up being bunked together, sitting at the same table together, and forced to spend every single day together. At summer camp, the person you hate the most ends up being the person you're most likely going to be paired with. Don't let the councilors know how much you hate someone; they are bound to make sure you get to know each other. Usually, when you hate something about another person, it is because they reflect a trait you hate about yourself.

We both had eating disorders, had experienced being molested, and our parents had shipped us off to summer camp because they didn't want to deal with us for whatever reason. Her family came from the rich part of town and were divorced. Mine lived in the crap part and never saw each other. We were never going to be friends; we were sure of it. That was until she forced me to eat, and I made her stop throwing up. We started talking about how we had fallen for the people who harmed us and the years of abuse we endured. We discovered we had far more in common than we didn't. When school started again, we were friends, and nothing the third friend could say was going to stop us from talking and getting to know each other more. Almost thirty years later, Celeste is still in my life. We always find some way to catch up and continue like no time has passed even if it's been years between visits. We've just been through so much together; there's no way of ending this friendship.

Flirtatious Little Sister

I was the youngest of three, and my brothers were always a bit different. Stevie was unpredictable to say the least. As I got older, I avoided spending time with him as much as possible. I had to avoid the physical altercations. Stevie had also started self-medicating. I really enjoyed annoying Sebastian because he always had his group of friends, and I loved playing up the little sister act. *I mean what cute little sister would not enjoy having the older boys looking at her? Especially knowing they will not do anything.*

I began spending time hanging out with my brother's friends whenever I had the chance. I wore large T-shirts and just my panties when I knew they were coming around to go fishing or something. I'd walk into the kitchen and get myself a bowl of cereal as if it was normal behavior. It really was; I never cared if anyone was there or not when I walked around the house. I just made sure I put a little extra attention to brushing my hair before I got my breakfast if the boys were around. Then I'd go get dressed and tag along with whatever plans I felt were intriguing enough for my attention. Sometimes, it was just hanging out and doing nothing; most of the time, I only saw the group for a few minutes here and there since I was now twelve going on thirteen, and they were getting ready for high school graduation.

I did make sure if they were hanging around the house, I made my presence known. I flirted with whomever I could. My brother would bring a new boy around, and I had to see if he thought I was cute. Most of them did. Jacob would notice pull the guy aside, and the flirting would end. Until Chad, for whatever reason, they did not care how much I flirted with him. He was completely safe to hang out with and spend my time and energy flirting. I learned about the band Queen. We talked about cute boys and crushes. Hanging out together for hours, we really got to know each other.

One day, he was at my house, waiting for a ride home. It was just after dark, and rain had just started to fall. We were talking like every other day; he was my friend. He stood over a head taller than me; he leaned down and kissed me gently. Pulling away, I kissed him back. Then we were lost in the moment for what felt like an eternity. When we stopped kissing, we realized how romantic the moment was and that it was my first kiss. He couldn't resist at the moment, and he said he had been thinking about kissing me for a while. We ended up kissing a lot after that. We hung out kissing on the couch, him touching my breasts and respecting me enough to never do anything else.

About six weeks later or so, we had grown tired of each other. We didn't need to keep going. The excitement had died down, and he met someone he really liked. He had to find out what was going to happen. I was happy for him because I really wasn't getting any great feelings from kissing him. I just loved the thrill of getting yelled at for kissing my brother's friend. Chad turned out to be gay; he never went any further with me because he just wasn't interested in me. He found me attractive as a person, but sexually, he didn't want me; he had a crush on a guy. We both had crushes on guys. I guess he was my first friend I kissed. It was a relationship based on friendship, and we did things together because we wanted to, where we addressed our human desires rather than our hormonal urges.

Fun Club

I was part of a group of teens who hung out together doing a bunch of things with a pair of adults. This was an after-school group, and we did a few summers together. Looking back now, it was for at-risk kids. During that time, I never really put any of the pieces together. We were all good kids. Some of us got into a little trouble here or there. Some of us had absent or abusive parents. I never saw myself as one of those kids at the time. I just thought we were a bunch of kids who got along and were doing things that kept us from getting into too much trouble.

We went roller-skating, to the movies, and on many adventures that we had to earn from participating in group activities we all hated at the time. Of course, as an adult, I don't remember what we did. I remember feeling Jaimiee was my friend, and all of us girls thought Kevin was "really hot." We were all crushed when he asked his long-time girlfriend to marry him. He was a nice man, and we were all jealous.

Over the summer work program, we had to participate in sex ed classes that had nothing to do with the one you take in school that tells you about how the body works. This one talked about your hormones and using protection. We talked about consent, abusive relationships, and alcohol and drug use and abuse. There were so many things we had to participate in with that program, which we all hated at the time. Yet looking back, it played an enormous role in me having my realization that I was one of those women.

I never would have realized I was a victim without knowing the signs of abuse. I never would have faced the reality that I was being manipulated by a narcissist if I was not forced to suffer through the classes we hated so much.

We would report in the morning to a classroom and learn basic job skills for a few hours. Which was the easiest part of the day. Then we had to go into groups for the embarrassing class where we discussed sex, abuse, drugs, and everything none of us wanted to discuss in an open room. By the end of the summer, we were completely comfortable talking about condoms and drugs like it was cookies and milk.

After our mornings in this strange building that later turned into an alternative high school, we went to our individual jobs throughout the town. My first year, I worked at a pet store. I learned about "pinkies," and that was probably the worst part of the job, even worse than cleaning up after kittens and puppies all summer.

Once every few weeks, we had our big trip day, and that's when we had the most fun. A friend of mine reminded me that we had gone on one of the trips, and some of the boys who were friends got into a fight over goddess knows what. One of them had their glasses get broken, and Kevin had to pay to have them replaced. The three boys were on suspension for a while.

This was definitely a group of misfits. We made jokes about it at the time, but I never saw how broken we all were back then. I am so glad we had Jaimiee and Kevin to help us learn the skills that later saved my life.

Losing My Brothers

In the group, there was my oldest brother, his best friend whom I'll call Jacob, his younger brother Noah, and then a bunch of random teenage boys I don't remember. Jacob was always like the big brother I wished my brother was; he protected me, looked out for me, and checked in with me. He knew if I was having a bad day or if I just needed to hang out. Noah wasn't really like a brother to me; he was always a friend. We crushed on each other for a while, but it never worked out, and that is completely okay because the universe had a plan that did not include us ever having that kind of relationship.

When Jacob signed up to go to boot camp, before he left, my mother wanted to make sure he had every possible tool he would need for every occasion. She had a dinner party with the fine china and every plate and piece of silverware. She wanted the young men to know when at an event like this, which fork to reach for without feeling as if they didn't belong. All the young men were there for their graduation dinner. I got to be involved, and I got to wear something that made me look like a girl for the first time in a long time. These young men were accustomed to seeing me dressed as the little sister in her brother's hand-me-down clothes.

I do not remember how many courses my mother served. This dinner felt like it went on forever. We had to use special napkins in a specific way. Our manners were top-notch. The boys were not allowed to make any remarks about anything that was not appropriate dinner talk. It was a very amusing experience even though the actual details are gone from memory.

I miss having Jacob as my brother. He's the one I would talk to when things were bad. He's the brother I trusted growing up, whom I felt was my actual brother even though it was never by blood. Jacob was the one who protected me from every young man. He may not realize how much of an impact his existence in my life really had on me during those years.

Sebastian had his own traumatic events during his lifetime. He has issues and a backstory that is not mine to share. The information I am going to share is just because it affects me and my relationship with him as he was never the kind of brother who looked out for me growing up, and I never had a good relationship with him. This happened after his best friend left for his military career, following his dream.

I loved playing video games; Sebastian had the gaming system in his bedroom. On this particular day, it was after my breasts had come in. I had long been missing the attention David had been giving me and in search for any version of it. Sebastian asked me to show him my breasts if I wanted to play the game. I was back in that room, back in that situation. I never thought my own brother would be just like him. I guessed this was normal. I was immediately pulled back to the child I had been as if I never left that moment in my life. I agreed because I felt that this was what you are supposed to do for your brother. He said it was like I was a magazine for him. He wasn't going to do anything.

I offered to help him as I was accustomed to doing and placed my hand near his member. Moments passed, he realized what had happened and stopped. He grabbed a blanket and kicked me out. From that day forward, he never looked at me again. Sebastian avoided being alone with me for any reason. We never spoke about it until the day I told him I forgave him for me.

I had officially lost two brothers, one to the Navy and one to life circumstances.

Getting into High School

By the time we got into high school, it seemed like every single one of my friends had a boyfriend. Yet none of the boys I thought were cute or wanted anything to do with me. The boys that did want my attention had been my bullies just a few months earlier. One of them, Mike, I had known since we were in preschool together, and he would tease me about the bloomers my mother had made me wear with every single one of my dresses because she didn't want anyone to see my underwear. "You have to be a proper little girl if you're going to climb at least wear these." On the monkey bars, shaped like a huge metal cage igloo, he said something about me wearing a diaper. *Wham!* I popped him in the face. He fell to the ground screaming in pain, bleeding. I broke his nose. There was no way in hell he was going to be the first boy I kissed. I didn't think he was cute in any way, and I was never going to let that event go. Even now, I find it one of the most amusing events in my childhood because we were four, and he thought he was better than me. He kept those airs about himself, and I was the only person who knew exactly how to keep him humble.

I liked to do things looking for attention when I was not in school. I changed my behavior to things that were no longer illegal. I was fifteen by now; I started to turn more toward boys because I was finally understanding my curves. My school was filled with boys I grew up with. I disliked all of them; just three years earlier, they were complete jerks. The ones who were not were best friends of the ones who had been. I wanted to meet a guy that had no ties to my history.

I would flirt with someone who went to a different school. I began going to dances at another school when one friend moved from our public regular school to the vocational school across town. I was hoping I would meet someone there. I began going to the football games and never met anyone. I was great at flirting, but I was horrible at making the first move. I was shy until I got talking.

Once I started talking to someone, the person I was in Alabama would come out, and I would become talkative. Most people saw me as the quiet, boy clothes–wearing Plain Jane girl because that's how I dressed. At school dances, I danced with my friends to the choreographed dances we had practiced time and time again until we knew all the steps.

Crowds of onlookers were astonished as four or five girls knew all the dance moves to most of the nineties' boy bands songs. We would start a train; the whole room would join in. I was right there next to the life of the party, and I loved it. No one knew me at those dances; they only knew me as the friend of Jen.

Jen was one of those girls who gave me her old clothes so I could dress like a female instead of only having my brother's old things. She was constantly getting new hairstyles and clothes. Her parents wanted to spend time with her. She lost friendships because she thought the girls had crushes on her brother. Our friendship ended for other reasons, reasons that happen between teenage girls who are just jerks.

We used to watch her brother play in his rock band. He could play anything on his electric guitar just by hearing it. The talent he has is amazing. We went to one of the events he was playing. Their mother told us not to leave our drinks unattended. We never thought anything of it. I guess we went to the bathroom or something.

After the show, she was acting really strangely. Her brother and his friends took her somewhere. I do not know what happened after that for her. I walked home alone. We never spoke again. I was upset and abandoned by another person I trusted in my life. Jen never knew my secrets. Most people had no idea why I kept to myself.

When we went back to school, she told everyone I was upset because she did not want to have sex with me or something. I told everyone she was a lesbian in retaliation. In the nineties, that was a big deal. Now who the hell cares? Love is love!

The most memorable thing in my freshman year of high school is how I discovered my spiritual beliefs. I was fifteen when I decided I was a pagan. I did not know what the word for my spiritual beliefs were. I knew my entire life what I believed and how I felt about God and everything that goes along with it.

Our history teacher let me do a report on any historical event I wanted to after I had completed all of the required work plus some. I chose the Salem Witch Trials. I have always felt like I am connected in some way. I spent every study hall and possible moment available in the library looking for books or information that would give me any type of information on the events. Then I had to take the route of "What if witchcraft is real?

This was like opening a can of worms. I was lost in the realm of Scott Cunningham and everything Wiccan. I was not sure about being a witch or witchcraft. I was unsure about being Wiccan. I was sure I was a dirt-worshipping, multigod-following pagan. I had found my religion. I had found the thing I felt when I was a little girl and I was looking up at Chief Rainbow, wishing I could be just like him.

I made my report, slightly different from my original plan, better because I followed the way the information pulled me instead of just sticking to the vague topic. When my classmates discovered I had done a report on witchcraft and dark arts, they assumed my black clothes and dark makeup meant I was evil. I kept reading, going deeper and deeper into the world. Knowledge is power; I needed to gain power.

I learned about paganism, Wicca, and the world of everything occult. My classmates began to really fear me. No one was bullying me anymore because they thought I would do something horrible to them. This is also around the time the movie *Craft* came out, and a lot of people thought that the movie witches was how real witchcraft worked.

Broken Brother

Over the years, even with Jacob around, Sebastian had his girl-friend, Lissa, around. She was his on-again, off-again heartbreak. He met her when he was about twelve. With our father's love story in our heads, we had unrealistic expectations of love. Our mother was his one and only. Our mother never told us her side of the story, and she loved his version.

Lissa introduced Sebastian to Tony. He needed a job; my father and brother were looking for summer help. He was average-looking, nothing really special about him except that he was my brother's friend and my father hated him. Tony worked very little at the worksites, and his employment did not last very long that summer. He was a waste of money and an irritating jerk. Tony listened to music my father hated. My father had no problem voicing his opinion when his radio station had been changed without permission.

I hung out with my brother, his girlfriend, and Tony, never alone. I figured when school started and Tony went back to his normal life and no longer worked with my brother and father in the business, that was the end of him. I was never going to see him again. I didn't care; I just enjoyed annoying my brother and father because he got under my father's skin, and I wanted attention. I never wanted to go out with this guy; he was a jerk.

Upon My Sixteenth Year

My mother and I had a ritual of going to Taco Bell for my birthday dinner. It was the closest thing I had ever had to a birthday party of any kind my entire life with my birthday falling the day after Christmas. This year, my father joined us for the first time that I can remember. To my surprise, Tony was working in the kitchen. I was sixteen. New Year's was the following week, and we had met over the summer. Who knew what the next year would bring? He would make a good first boyfriend—date him a little bit and get my father to notice me. Maybe he finally would want to spend time with me. That was my plan; unfortunately, life never goes as you want.

My best friend, Celeste, and I went to the New Year's town party, 1999 going into 2000. The world was supposed to end, and this was going to be when everything was over. We had a great time doing things that sixteen-year-old girls do, running around, laughing. We talked to friends, checked in with her dad, and we sang Spice Girls karaoke. "First night" was filled with laughs, memories, bright lights, fireworks, and karaoke. At some point in the night, Tony found us and joined in our good natured fun. He was my first kiss of the New Year.

The next day, Tony came out to Celeste's house, and the three of us went hiking together. As the next few months went on, I realized what she had said: He wasn't a good fit for me. We were dating for about three months, and I was ready to break up with him because for some reason, I was starting to pull away from my friends for him.

I don't remember him ever asking me to do it; I just remember doing it naturally.

Tony came over that night, climbing through the bedroom window because my father did not like him. My plan was set; tonight, I was going to tell Tony it was over. My mind was made up. I did not see my future with him. Three months was good for a first relationship. Everything had run its course, and I was confident in my decision.

As I began to form the words and tell him I was not seeing our relationship moving forward, he started smooth-talking. He started kissing me. He moved to my neck, to the place he knew made me feel special. Tony moved his hand down to my crotch, kissing my neck and rubbing his hand against me. I told him I meant it, that we could not be together anymore. That it was over. Our relationship was done; I was breaking up with him.

Tony continued his kissing and smooth-talking until I no longer said no to him. Part of me was back in the bedroom with David. I was lost in the moment, lost in my mind, lost in thought. He had never touched me like this. This felt different than before; this was exciting. My body was responding to him in ways I seemed to have no control over. One part of my mind knew I should kick him out and our relationship was over; another side said I had to keep going.

We had sex that night—continuously. I had planned to break up with him, and somehow, he managed to get me to have sex. This meant I was stuck with him for at least a little bit longer. I refused to be one of those girls that were single the morning after losing her v-card. Many of my friends had that happen, but they were in love with the boys who did it to them. I was definitely not in love with him.

I went to Planned Parenthood. If I was going to have sex, I was going to be safe. I knew I was never going to be able to take a pill every single day. I opted to go on the depo vera shot. This meant every three months, I would go in for a booster, and if I missed the three months, it was good for up to four, and they had the month of overlapping to make sure the young woman was able to get it without having any problems. This was perfect; I could easily remember to get in there every three months, and I wouldn't have to worry about my parents finding some kind of birth control pills and throwing them away or having to explain myself.

Now that I was having sex, I was being responsible. I decided I was going to start having some fun. This meant a few different things to me at sixteen. I was going to start to push the envelope and see what kind of things the world had to offer me.

Looking back, the behavior may have been fed by Tony. He had been able to have me withdraw from my family because they caused me pain. I withdrew from my friends because I did not trust them. I was alone except for when I was with him. If he asked me to do something, I was probably going to do it. If he suggested something in jest, I would likely build on the idea, making it my own. The only people we hung out with were the people he chose to spend time with; the quality of his friends were not the same as the ones I had given up. I never saw it at the time.

I brought Tony to tour my high school, thinking he was going to come and finish with my class. While I was giving him a tour, we stopped by Celeste's classroom, and her teacher told us to "get the fuck out of her school." We did exactly that. I showed him down the hallway, down the stairs, and out the door. I never walked back into the building. Now we were free to have adventures doing whatever we wanted because I no longer had any responsibilities, and my friends didn't want me around because he was always someone they never trusted, and I couldn't understand why.

Unleash the Crazy

Each day had an adventure of its own. Sometimes, it was just hanging out with his friends or alone. We would do something unremarkable. I journaled and drew a lot. Then there were some memories that I have got to include. These are the ones that are insane, and I am amazed I turned into the person I am as an adult.

Tony only had older friends. They all knew how to have one kind of fun, the troublesome kind.

I tried pot for the first time. We were in his backyard with a group of five or six of us. His little sister was there, and she lit up the joint. Britney took a drag, held it in, and passed it to the next person. They repeated the action, going on and on until it reached me. I took a small drag, and I immediately began to cough. I thought I was going to die as my lungs began to tighten. The smoke had closed my bronchial tubes, and I was having an asthma attack. I was unable to breathe. The group began laughing immediately, thinking I was just a newbie and I had taken too big of a hit. I was sure I was going to die as I had to search my bag for my emergency inhaler, unsure if I was ever going to find it and feeling as though I was going to pass out from the lack of oxygen.

There was a dance place with a bar that was open to underage people one day a week. We were regulars there. They had a disco bar and great music for dancing. We would go with a group of like eight to fifteen people. I would bring Celeste whenever she was able to come. We had a habit of getting these little glow-in-the-dark mouth sticks. Celeste and I would lock our mouths and switch the glow sticks from one mouth to the other and show the men we were with what we had done, having fun while teasing the opposite sex. We had perfected our flirtation by now. We knew exactly how to make a man go from zero to OMG instantaneously. Celeste and I had a lot of fun kissing in public just because we were best friends, and that's what we did to make guys look at us. We really enjoyed the attention.

Tony liked to see how far he could get me to go; he put me into positions I would never put myself into. He wanted me to try threesomes. The first one was with Celeste. I cannot remember who suggested we bring her into the mix. We were already kissing. I was already having sex with Tony. Why not have Celeste join? I trusted her with everything already.

Celeste and I discussed this, and she agreed. Tony was allowed to touch her, use his mouth on her, but intercourse was off-limits. I went back to Tony, and he agreed to her terms. *I mean, what kind of man would disagree with this?* We had really only committed to trying something new. He was excited to be able to have sex with me and have the ability to look at two beautiful naked women at the same time.

When we got to my bedroom, we confirmed the guidelines and set out the plan. Celeste was uncomfortable with touching parts, and I had never tried it. Celeste trusted me, and I was somehow responsible for this whole experience. I also had a little bit of amateur experience back with Lizzie that no one knew about. I sure as hell was never going to tell anyone about that. Yet here I am in my tell-all tale... telling everything about my life. I have always said I am an open book. Pick an age—I will tell you my traumatic experience.

Celeste and I began by kissing each other and then included Tony. We moved down to his member and got him started before paying more attention to one another again, removing each other's clothes and putting on a nice show as we did. I kissed her neck and moved down to her chest, massaging her breasts and kissing her nipples in all the ways I liked myself. I had Celeste lie on her back as I kissed her down her stomach and had her spread her legs and moved my hand down to her special place very few people have been before me. I rubbed the little button as I kissed her mouth. She kissed me back, trying to rub mine just as nicely and failing to make me feel anywhere as nice as I could do for her.

I stopped her from touching me and moved my mouth down to the space between her legs, kissing, licking, rubbing, and doing everything I knew would make her feel amazing. I placed my fingers inside her, curling just a little while thrusting my hand back and forth and her body reacting to each movement I made with my mouth and hand until she lost complete control. I had found the spot that made her go crazy, the spot so many men have no idea how to find, yet I was a professional at finding it on my first try.

As Celeste climaxed, a jolting full-body expression of my success, I knew I had done exactly what I had set out to do. Now I would turn my attention toward Tony. He had been trying desperately to do to me what I had been doing to her, but he was failing miserably in comparison to my success. I moved up to his face, kissing his mouth with mine. He watched what I had been doing, and he was more turned on than ever before. Tony didn't need much from me as I straddled him and placed him inside me, finishing him and having the two people I had set out to give pleasure completely satisfied at my whim.

This gave me a sense of power. I did not enjoy it the way I liked other things. I felt like it was a chore. I completed the task at hand, and I had no regrets. I made a choice; I enjoyed the moment and excitement that came along with the event. I loved the way I felt when I was giving someone pleasure. I wanted to chase the high I felt from giving someone else the joy I gave her. It was something that made me feel better than anything I had felt before. I allowed Tony to have more control over my actions and behavior. I was chasing a high I could only feel with sex.

Tony brought me to one of his friends' houses. They were having a party, and he wanted me to go. We were going to be spending the night. This was a place where I had met many of the people, and he was hoping it would turn into a group orgy. I did not know that was his plan. Tony gave me a few drinks and something else; I do not quite remember everything from the evening. I believe he had drugged me; the night still remains a squiggly memory. It flashes in and out, parts of it, like watching an old projector film that's been poorly spliced together.

They had two large black leather couches put together in an L-shape. Tony and I sat together talking. A group of his friends scattered the room, smoking, drinking, and talking until we all started to get tired, everyone going to their "assigned sleeping arrangements." Tony's friend, one of the guys I had met multiple times before, came and sat next to us on one of the couches.

It was now time to pull out the pillows and blankets. I sat with Tony on one side, Jamie on the other. Jamie was known for having a lot of sexual partners. He was a hotshot as far as anyone knew and for what he let everyone believe. Tony wanted to share me with him. I was unsure because I did not know Jamie, and I only had one sexual partner. I did not say no; I told them we could try and see how far things went.

We sat down, kissing and touching and my hands on both men. We moved to the floor. I never had intercourse with Jamie. I made sure both men fell asleep satisfied; it was the least I could do since I was at least responsible for their sexual tension. The next day, I gave Jamie another hand job because we were there together and he asked.

To me, hand jobs were like candy. If a guy was nice to me and my boyfriend knew about it, there was no problem. Jamie was literally put into my hand by Tony, so this was not a problem. Tony's sister, Britney, did not agree. She was one of the people at the party the night before. She came out of the bedroom the next day, found us on the couch, then told her brother I was cheating on him. From there, it is a bit of a fog as I had given hand jobs to a few different men at Tony's request, in the back seat of cars, at a theater, on the roof of an old building. *I was very irresponsible with my hands.*

Adding Excitement

When those sexy adventures became dull, Tony switched things up with a group of three friends who had not been around in the beginning, Sam, Paul, and Victor. Sam had this really nice little red five-seater car that looked like some kind of sports car. I didn't care what it was because it fit all five of us on the occasions we all wanted to go hang out. We spent a lot of time going to the mall or just going on drives. Tony still worked at Taco Bell, and his friends all had some kind of jobs as far as I knew. I kept doing my own thing and honing my artistic abilities because I had earned a free ride to art school in Colorado a few years earlier. I just had to finish school and turn eighteen to use it—if I didn't go into the military. I was still trying to figure out what I wanted to do because I never expected to be kicked out of school, and I had no idea how to tell my parents. Some of the adventures we had were unbelievable, and I don't know how I didn't die or end up in jail.

On a whim, Tony, Sam, and I got into the tiny red car and decided we were going to go to Bangor Maine to try to run into Stephen King, Tony's favorite author. I was always up for an adventure so of course I had to go. We grabbed a few bags of clothes and wrote down the directions and started driving. I was exhausted; the back seat was too small to fall asleep so I folded down the back and opened the trunk and fell asleep. I was essentially asleep in the trunk; my pillow was our duffel bag and I was comfortable because I actually had space to lay out and sleep during this extremely long ride.

I woke up to men screaming in French because green means stop. We had crossed the Canadian border because they took the wrong exit miles before. It was exciting, scary, and really dangerous. The group of men had guns pulled on us, yelling at everyone to get out of the car. I had my identification card with me because I always did. We were scolded and called "Stupid Americans" with a heavy French accent then sent away. I learned their speed limit signs are in kilograms, and green means stop in Canada, two things I never knew before that day. We never made it to Maine; we went back to our tiny state and continued other adventures.

Tony had a friend, Milly, a bit older than us. She was married to a nice man; they had three kids and a fourth on the way. I discovered later there is a pretty good chance that the child was actually his. The two of them, Milly and Tony, had a strange relationship. They were friends and did rituals together.

We had many nights at their house. I only remember feeling afraid, unsure, and overwhelmed as if they were lying about everything metaphysical that was happening. I played along because I was used to that kind of mental health issue with my brother. When Stevie had a schizo episode, it was best for me to go along with it. Anytime I did not, he turned me into one of the bad guys and attacked me as a result. This was about self-preservation.

One day, Sam decided she wanted to start dating Victor. The thing about Sam is that she didn't tell Victor that she was mid transition and hadn't had her male parts removed. When they hooked up, Victor thought he was with a woman, and he was one of the happiest men I had met. I kept asking Sam how it was possible to be intimate and hide something like that from Victor. I still don't know the answer, and I don't want to know. I'm happy to be left in the dark. I think that was a very dishonest and horrible thing Sam did to him. I ended up breaking the news to Victor later on when Sam refused to tell him herself.

I think that might be the day that Sam got really upset and decided to go on a really crazy joyride in that little red car. I was the passenger, and I was the person she wanted to talk to about her bad day. I don't remember what we talked about for most of the day. I remember it was late, most of the stores were closed, and she was speeding around the town going the wrong way on one-way streets and then got onto the highway speeding over 120 mph. We got back to the condo where the guys were, and I was shaking. Victor was probably twenty-five or so and had been supplying alcohol for everyone, and I was the only one who didn't drink. That night, I downed three spritzers like it was nothing. I thought I was going to die, and I wanted to kill Sam for putting me through that. I never let her drive with me in the car again.

The group of us went somewhere a few days later, another joyride. We stopped for gas. This was the first time I remember being in the car when we filled the tank. I never thought anything of it; we always had a full tank. Tony was driving, Sam in the passenger seat, Victor to my left, me in the middle, and Paul, Sam's brother to my right, all three of us in the back row. We were filling the tank to go somewhere, but I don't remember what the plan was. Sam was filling the tank when Paul said something to get Tony's attention. Tony looked at the attendant through the window, Sam stopped pumping the gas, and the two of them got back into their seats before Tony started the car and drove off. The roads were wet from rain, and he was in a rush. Sirens were blaring in the distance, and he was sure they were on the way for us.

Apparently, the group of four were stealing gas from different locations for months, and I had no clue. As Tony was trying to avoid the impending disaster, he swerved around a line of cars that had stopped at the light just before the on ramp. Missing the turn, he slammed on the brake and tried to make it back to where he had intended to bring us. Instead, we landed into the cement wall of the on ramp, the engine block on Tony's lap. Sam opened her door and crawled out onto the ground as her brother was yelling at her to move. He kicked the seat forward and started dragging Tony from his seat under the engine; no airbags had gone off. I had curled into a ball as soon as I felt the danger. On my way, I kicked Paul's foot and sprained his ankle and kicked Sam in the kidney. Victor wasn't wearing his seat belt and ended up hooking his ear on the hanger above his window.

Once all five of us were outside the car; we looked at the car, evaluated our own physical damages, and decided we had to get to the hospital. It was up the hill from where we were. We decided to start walking. It was before cell phones, and we didn't know if that car was going to explode because it looked like it was going to the way there was a small flame inside the engine and we had just filled the tank. We were too afraid to stay there and risk being blown up. The risk of walking to the hospital outweighed the risk of staying and waiting for help.

We made it about a quarter mile before a police car rolled up and asked us if we were involved in the accident. This is where I discovered that the car was stolen. The gas had been stolen for months, the plates were also stolen from another car, and the brother who was so adamant about us leaving the scene was on parole. I sat in the back seat of the cruiser, completely shocked and physically unharmed as I was surrounded by people I thought I knew. Tony asked me to marry him, and I thought he was going along with the ride like me.

My Arrest

My parents were on their twenty-fifth wedding anniversary trip. They were gone for about ten days. Sebastian was supposed to be in charge of keeping the house safe because they knew Tony was a bad person. He had already done bad things to me by now, and I was already saved at least once. They only knew about the mental abuse because Tony had succeeded in pulling me away from my family and friends over the past six or so months.

Stevie was self-medicating, getting stoned, drunk, or both depending on the moment. My parents could not count on him for anything. He had dropped out of school. Sebastian was only worried about Lissa. I broke the rules and let Tony into the house after I thought it was empty. We hung out for a while in my bedroom until I decided to go into the bathroom or the kitchen.

I was immediately met with Stevie and his instantaneous rage. He threw a few punches and grabbed my throat. When I awoke, the neighbors had called the police because they heard screaming as though someone was going to die. I was the only person under age. The two of them had restraining orders put on each other, and I was brought to the police station and set in a holding cell until arrangements could be made.

That was the best day of my life to that point. The officers were unable to reach my parents, my oldest brother, or my grandmother. I was completely alone except for my boyfriend and intoxicated abusive brother who had given me bruises and scratches along my neck and jaw. I should have been feeling remorse, sadness, or anything other than relief as they removed the metal cuffs from my bound wrists and gently escorted me into the empty cell.

A metal toilet, two metal boards holding thin pads they considered to be a mattress on top of each other attached to the wall, and a tiny basin for a sink is all that was in the room. One wall was just bars, a camera looking in the room, and a two-way speaker. The room should have felt cold, dreary, meant for a criminal. I felt safe.

For the first time in my entire life, for as long as I could remember, I felt completely safe. They supplied a pillow, a lightweight blanket, and a meal while I was sleeping securely. I could not keep my eyes open. It was as if all the stress I had been carrying my entire life had been taken away. I did not care if this was going to be for one day or even a month. I was on a vacation from my real life. This was the best day of my life. I wanted to stay here.

The door opened; I was released to Celeste's mother. She never liked me and made sure I felt the unwelcome of being her problem until my parents' return. As soon as Tony showed up with his friend in their red car, I left. It was the only choice. I could not ruin my best friend's life since her mother already thought I had done that to my own. I walked away and could not look back.

Carny

Shortly after, Tony and I got jobs with the carnival in town. They let me work at sixteen and offered to bring me along with them for the season. I wanted to keep having adventures. I could not think of an excuse to turn it down. I would be in charge of taking tickets at the bounce house. I would not have to set up, test rides, or take anything down. During the day, I got to explore different cities, and enjoy each place and just have a little fun. I was paid in cash. I had full freedom I would not have had if I had stayed where I was. I would go to sleep on Sunday in the trailer and wake up in a new place while everyone else was beginning to start setting up again. It was an exciting experience as much as it was scary.

The men did not speak much English; they spoke only Spanish. I remember one day, I got out of the trailer, and they made breakfast. I came out covered in bruises. It was one of the first times he hit me. The Spanish men brought him away. I was afraid of the men. I was afraid of the situation. I was afraid to call my parents. I was afraid to be alone. Eventually, I decided to call my parents and have them pick us up because the fear was too much. I had never felt crushing fear from every direction before.

It was really cool to wake up on the beach and walk along the boardwalk in a place I had no idea where I was with a carnival that no longer exists. I am glad my parents came and picked me up that day. The very next carnival, they set up, and during the testing, a bolt broke on the Ferris wheel, and the entire thing came crashing down and killed the operator in the process. I think it was the universe saving my life as one of my dear friends was still working for them and knew the young man.

I got home, and I decided to get my first tattoo. My neighbor was back from Florida and staying with his mother. He didn't know my age, and I was really good at telling half-truths. So I told him I was underage and my birthday was in December. I just didn't say which year I would be turning eighteen. I wanted a rose on my left shoulder blade to match my grandmother, the woman I had called when I got my first period, the woman who beat cancer, the same woman who gave my father life. With a little conversation, flirting, and talking about a tattoo he gave himself in a very outlandish location, I had my tattoo. Over two decades later, I still love it just as much today as I did the day I got it.

Life Change

Every day of my relationship with Tony, I never knew if we were going to be together or not. One day I was the best thing that happened to him, and the next thing we were broken up. He would be with me for a while and leave again for days or weeks, and I just kept letting him come and go whenever he wanted because he had this power over me. I wanted to be with him, but I lost my virginity to him. I loved him, or at least I thought I loved him.

I kept track of my birth control, and I was always very diligent. I went in to get my third or fourth dose, and instead of the regular visit, I discovered I was pregnant. All of the dangerous behavior I was practicing was going to stop. I was no longer going to hang out with the friends who were drinking and having fun. I was no longer going to do things just because it sounded like fun at the time. I had to figure out how to be a mother because I was on birth control, and things like this don't just happen when you're being careful. It turned out that the shot I had received three months earlier had failed after a month. I was already more than eight weeks pregnant, and by the time I got to the OB for the first time, there was a heartbeat. I didn't know anything about abortions; I only knew that my parents were completely against them and that I had to carry it, and I was now going to be a mother.

My entire life changed in under two minutes. Tony did not understand the importance of making lifestyle changes. I was now committed to being a better parent than I had ever had. I was not going to be hanging out with any of his questionable friends or doing any of the questionable things. When he told his mother and sister I was pregnant, they said it wasn't his baby. His sister was convinced I was messing around with other guys because Tony had other women I didn't know about. He had fathered other children. My parents were ecstatic to step up and be what I needed as I was forced into adulthood. I began going to parenting classes, and I got my GED. I graduated eighteen months before the rest of my original class.

My parents signed the paperwork to have me marry Tony, although the night before, I was ready to back out. I was nine months pregnant, and I knew I didn't want to spend my life with him. They said it was too late and basically chorused me into my marriage. I put on a happy face, and I married the man who spent time in jail for pulling a knife on his mother's landlord while I was pregnant.

When my little girl was born, I had already known everything important about what I had to do to keep her safe and provide for her. I was bringing her to playgroups, and I had a visiting person who made sure I stayed up to date with everything so that I did not mess her up. I went to work at 4:00 a.m. because the monetary burden was too much for my parents, and I wanted to help them. I worked for a few days before I came home at 7:00 a.m. to a newborn baby screaming in pain as she had soaked through her diaper and the man who was responsible for taking care of her was still sound asleep. I stopped working; I could not trust him to take care of her. I never left him alone with my baby again if I was not close by.

My graduation was a few weeks after she was born, and I had us ready to go without a problem. Tony wanted to go, but for whatever reason, he made us late. I missed the speech, and they were planning to give me a scholarship to college. I kicked him out of our house because this was an important moment in my life, and he had ruined it. Again and again, he was coming and going. I was getting my life with my daughter moving in a good direction, and he showed up just long enough to throw me off-kilter and disappear again.

The First Letdown

When my baby was three months old, he wanted to take her out to visit his friends, and I was not allowed to go with him. I had heard from the rumor mill that he was hanging out with another woman whom he had a baby with before my daughter was born. It was possible these kids would be siblings. This other person was not a good parent, and neither was Tony. I couldn't trust him when I was around; how would I trust him if I wasn't? I refused to let him take her, and I remember holding her, running to the living room, fear fueling me. Handing my three-month-old baby over to my mother, I told her sternly, "Go lock the two of you in your room and call the police." I was almost on my knees as I was protecting her with my entire body from this man who had hurt me many times before. I refused to let him hurt my child.

My mother locked the two of them in her bedroom, and I kept myself between Tony and the door. There was a lot of yelling and hitting as I protected my daughter with everything I had. I just kept telling my mother to keep the door locked and call for help. I kept screaming, "Call the cops!" as pain and panic overcame me with each blow he delivered. My mother never did make that call. I ended up covered in bruises with three broken ribs. We never told anyone what really happened that day. Tony decided to leave when he realized no amount of hitting and kicking me was going to get him the baby he wanted.

The state services kept telling me I had to stop allowing him back. Until I was finally ready to cut all ties with him, they were not going to be able to really help me get out of the situation I was in. This was a cycle of abuse. I did not want to admit it to myself or anyone else. I was being hurt mentally, sexually, and physically by this man. He had a hold on me that only a person who has lived through it can understand. The cycle kept going on and on. I kept falling for his words, and I kept letting him back into my life where he would do another thing that was catastrophically worse than the time before.

Parenting Classes

———————

After I had my daughter, I was told by child protective services I would have a few choices. My new husband had spent time in jail for pulling a knife on his mother's landlord. I learned this from a social worker instead of from him. I had assumed he was cheating on me again as he was a serial cheater.

The Department of Children and Families wanted both of us to attend parenting classes to make sure we knew how to properly care for and provide everything necessary for our newborn child. I jumped at the opportunity to become the best possible mother. I accepted every resource they offered me, and I participated in any program that had any possibility of helping my daughter strive for her growth and development.

I was bound and determined to be the best possible mother I could be. Every single week, I reported to my social worker. We tracked my daughter's developmental progress, set small goals for myself, and we talked about what I was doing and what I needed to do next.

This taught me how to make large goals and then break them into smaller goals. I had never had goals before. I had never seen my goals come to fruition. She kept every one of my goal tracker sheets from the beginning until I finished working with her. When we went back to the beginning, we were almost amazed to see my progress.

Tony was not as receptive to the idea of taking guidance in a world he knew nothing about. They tried to convince him with different reasons for joining their fathers' group. They were men who just talked about their partners, venting about their partners. They shared stories about their kids. The men also talked about their addictions and other subjects that the man in charge could not share with me. I never told Tony any of the information I was given. He went to three total classes and was completely against going again.

Later when things happened, each of our choices during this time played a major role in everything else.

I had learned how to discipline my child without using violence or anger. I learned how to do the daily care you usually learn when you're a child and your parents have you brushing your own teeth, showering daily, and taking care of yourself. My own parents did not do that. They were absent parents. I was not going to be that type of parent.

I met a woman who was in a custody battle, trying to get her children back from foster care. She had chosen drugs, alcohol, and men over her own children multiple times. The same program that was working with me had been working with her for a lot longer. She decided to start making changes only after the children were taken out of her custody. I was being proactive and making the changes and learning things before I made any major mistakes.

That woman never completed the program and never regained custody, and I never heard anything from her again after I finished that class. I was able to leave it early because I was doing everything and participating more than they had expected anyone to do. I took everything they had been telling us extremely seriously, and I was not willing to take any chances on losing my baby.

This is where I discovered that I could not allow Tony to be alone with my daughter. He brought her out on a day trip once and brought her back in the same diaper. I marked the back inside of each diaper with a marker so I knew if he had changed her at all. She was overflowing, filthy, and starving. All the snacks I packed for her were gone. I assume he had eaten them because she was covered in what looked like a popsicle. That was the first and last time he brought her anywhere without me.

The Kidnapping

When my daughter was about a year old, he had been stalking the house. He broke in after everyone had finally left me home with her alone for the first time in weeks or months. I was living in fear by now; I couldn't go outside alone. I do not remember every detail of that afternoon. I remember he hit me after I refused to let him take her. I lost consciousness, awaking to see him leaving with my baby and no car seat. I was sure I would never see my child again.

In a distraught state of mind, I took pills from the medicine cabinet then lay in my bed, waiting to die. I began to think about my baby girl, everything that monster was going to put her through, how much she was going to hate me for taking the easy way out, how much he had already hurt me, and what he was likely going to do to her. I needed to fight. I called 911, and I told them what I did. Just then, my mother pulled into the driveway. I handed her the phone as I began to get very sleepy.

I woke up in the hospital, tubes attached to me. They made me drink a disgusting charcoal liquid that made me sick from both ends. I spent two nights in the ICU. Police and child protective services interviewed me between restless naps. I found out that Tony was downstairs with alcohol poisoning while I was upstairs, and the baby was nowhere to be found.

My mother was supposed to go to his mother's house with the police to pick her up. She was too afraid of my in-laws. I did not see my baby girl for three days as my brother-in-law had my daughter. I went to his house when I was released, and he told me he was keeping her safe for me.

The next morning was the custody hearing. My brother-in-law held his side and brought my little girl. I was granted full custody. They all said that under the circumstances, I reacted the way anyone could have. The fact that I decided to fight and get help was a huge step in my favor, and I had to go into therapy to help with my mental health.

Over the next couple of months, I was going to therapy, taking care of my baby girl, bringing her to play groups, attending parenting groups, and doing everything I could to figure out what I needed to do to improve our lives. I was in a bad place. A lot of that time was spent in a fog of depression. I was still in denial about the abuse I was victim to.

The Rape

That August, I needed money to buy diapers, and Tony needed a place to stay because he was working at the carnival again. I let him sleep on my parents' couch against my better judgment. I put my daughter to bed with her normal routine. I told him the rules for staying at the house, and we agreed on boundaries. I went to bed locking my door after telling him he was not welcome in my bedroom. My daughter's crib was right next to my bed.

While I was asleep, he entered my bedroom. He crawled on top of me. I felt the terror as I was unable to scream for help. I could not wake the baby; she was not going to have this etched in her little subconscious. The pain was unbearable as he was twice my size and even stronger.

I could not breathe. I could not scream. I could not fight. I could not move. I was breaking under him. I had nothing left as tears fell down my face. I stopped fighting. I allowed him to finish, my entire body numb as I realized I was the same person I was ten years earlier. No one was going to protect me. I would never be safe. I had to protect that little girl. At least he was not going after her.

He left me lying there, a broken woman. I could not move for hours. The sun came up; I never fell asleep. I never moved. I just watched my sleeping baby, knowing that I did everything I could to keep her safe. I kept his mind off her. He had left, hopefully for a long time. At that moment, I never wanted to see him again.

A few weeks later, I found out I was pregnant again. I had been pushing my baby girl around in her stroller all day. I felt off in a way that was not illness. I walked into the pharmacy, afraid of what might be the fate ahead of me. I purchased a pregnancy test, realizing I had never actually done this before. I would have to read the instructions and hope I did not mess up.

I walked to the fast-food joint next door and entered the bathroom with the stroller. My entire body was shaking with a different kind of fear. I brought us into the handicapped stall, parking the stroller to face the corner and locking the door. I opened the box and read the instructions. Then I read them again.

Waiting for the results was the longest few minutes of my life. I probably could have been watching paint dry, and it would have taken less time than these two minutes. I watched as the little line made its way across the test section and passed the control line. I watched the faded line become more prominent as my mouth lost all ability to retain moisture. There was a demon spawn growing inside me. What the hell was I going to do?

For the first time in my life, I was now contemplating every option. I knew the options: abortion, adoption, keep. There are pros and cons to every single choice for every single person. Every single person has their own right to choose. I walked home, pushing the stroller with my baby girl, making a fair argument for each choice. I weighed pros and cons, going around and around trying to decide what was the best choice for me.

Abortion. Everything would be over right away, but I would be living my life knowing I had made that choice, a choice I may not regret at that moment. Who is to say I would not regret it in the future? Would my heart be able to survive making that choice, knowing that I could not do that with my daughter just a short time before?

Adoption. I could carry the baby full term and give it to a family that was searching for a child, similar to my own parents who were unable to conceive and wanted a family. Then when the children grew up, I would have to figure out how to explain to her how she had a younger sibling somewhere in the world. I would not know if the baby was in foster care or adopted, if the child had a good family or grew up in the system.

That left me with one option: I was keeping the baby. I got home, and I had to break it to my parents. I never told them the events of that night. I told them I debated the three options, and I was keeping it. My baby girl was going to be a big sister. My parents did not look disappointed or upset with me. They accepted the fact as it was, even appeared happy to have another baby arriving to our family.

Pregnancy

Tony called a few weeks later, I told him I was pregnant. He told me he was not the father, *Jerry Springer* television show style, and I hung up the phone, angry. That was the end of it for me. I never pressed charges. I made calls to the support services who had been waiting for me to make this choice. I was done with his roller coaster of emotions. I was not going to let this baby go through anywhere near the same kind of trauma that this little girl had experienced in her fourteenish months of life.

During my pregnancy, I had been using food to cope with everything. I just kept eating because when you're pregnant, you can use it as an excuse to eat even though it is not true. I gained over two hundred pounds with my second pregnancy. The emotional toll I was experiencing, I just did not know what to do. I could not deal with my emotions the way I had always done in the past. I was scared to death of going for walks because my mother had slipped once on the ice and lost the baby.

I was afraid of any physical activity because of the "what-ifs" that came with it. My mother had given me a ton of irrational fears that kept my mind full of more fear. I just kept gaining and gaining. I never talked about my pregnancy to anyone. The people in the play-group just thought I was getting fat. They were completely shocked when I showed up with a newborn one day. I never had a pregnancy glow, and I never bragged about him. I went to all my regular doctor appointments; I took care of everything I had to in order to keep him safe and healthy. I just refused to tell anyone how much was really going on with me.

Tony kept calling me to make arrangements to see her. He kept not showing up. I would waste my entire day waiting for him. He never called to let me know he was not coming. From September until December, I allowed him to have control of my Saturdays. I kept thinking he would show up when he made plans to see his daughter. He would say he would be there at noon. I would wait all day for him.

I gave him a two-hour window. I he did not show up in that period, he was not going to see her. If he came late, he lost the time. I was finished waiting on him. I finally put my foot down. When 2:00 p.m. came around, I was leaving no matter what. I had one of my parents bring us somewhere even if it was just a ride around the block. I needed it to appear that I had plans.

By January, he stopped calling completely and making false promises to see my baby daughter.

In April, the day I got home from the hospital, Tony was pissed that I put him on the birth certificate. It was the first time I had heard from him in over three months for anything other than fake plans. While he was yelling at me, I responded with one of my favorite responses. I told him, "I hate you. In fact, if you got hit by a Mac truck and were killed, I would sing at your funeral and dance on your grave." It was the first time I had ever stood up to him. I had never said anything like that to him. I was no longer fighting for myself; I was protecting my babies from this monster.

Daughter's Major Trauma

When Stevie came home from auto body school, he was very ill. Between mental illness and alcoholism, he was not himself. The brother I had was not the one I grew up with; he was also not the one I was able to have later in our lives.

This version of him was a painful man to be around. He was drinking too much every single day. He was smoking like a chimney. Stevie was not really my brother. Before he left, he got into drugs pretty badly, and as far as I knew, he was still that version of him.

I was nine months pregnant with my son. My father brought me up to the grocery store after I put my daughter to bed. She was asleep. He was supposed to be watching her. I did not realize he was incapable at the time. We walked into the grocery store, and the woman working at the service desk yelled as loud as she could that we needed to get home because my daughter had gotten bitten by a dog.

My father and I rushed home to find Sebastian holding my daughter and a blood-covered shirt over her face. I picked up my baby and carried her into my brother's truck as he said he would drive. The normal drive took half the amount of time, and as we sat in the seat, I remember telling my baby girl she was going to be okay. I got her to calm down, and the bleeding stopped.

We were seen right away, and a doctor stitched up her lip before we were bussed to the children's hospital, where the surgeon cleaned up my baby's face. He yelled out in the midst of the chaos to tell everyone, "Don't you dare let them put that dog down! This is a paw.

The dog did not bite this baby! He was trying to get away! This was an accident."

The nurses made me call my house to tell my father to make sure the dog was not put down. This was a complete freak accident; the dog was not to blame. My mother was sitting near the room while they were cleaning my daughter's face with a large syringe filled with saline. She saw it and passed out. Now I had two people I had to take care of in the hospital: my daughter from this freak dog accident and my mother because she thought there was a needle on the end of a syringe. I laughed at her for years over it.

The medical team was sure that I was going to go into labor. Why not have all three of us in a hospital bed by the time this whole thing was over? Even with all the stress of that night, my son was born about a month later, when he was induced because he really did not want to make an appearance on his own.

One Last Hit

I went to work at a department store in October 2003 after my second baby was born, my first son. I needed money, and I needed to start figuring out how to be a better mother. I was there for a little over three years. I experienced a few life-changing friendships and moments during that time.

Tony made his first appearance about a month after I finished my training as a front-end cashier. I hadn't heard from him since April; it was now almost Thanksgiving. I had thought he was done with me. I was wrong; he wanted to make sure I still knew he had a mental hold on me.

I was going about my regular work day, completely confident in my regular work day. I wore an oversized vest to cover my excess weight, hiding the person I had become and pretending I was confident. When I was behind the register, protected in my alcove, I was safe until Tony came to the end of my register and made his presence known.

Tony stood between the aisles, a shorter older woman by his side. She appeared much older than him. His arm was around her in a way he used to hold me. Something in me froze as he walked over to me and made threats about my son's name, birth certificate, and a promise to take my daughter one day. I was frozen in fear, the same fear I felt the last time he was anywhere near me, the same way I felt the night my son was created.

My manager noticed the ghostlike complexion I wore and my inability to move. Terri walked over to me, calling to me, unable to get my attention with words alone. She walked in front of me, understanding the trauma I had experienced. Terri had broken the trance I had no idea I was in. I was sent into the security room, where she told them what had happened.

The security team found him on the cameras right away. Someone brought the door watchers an image of Tony. They kept me in the accounting office until he was safely off the premises. Any time he showed up, if I was working, they sent me to another part of the store. My managers were really good at helping me avoid reliving the trauma. They wanted me to regain the confidence he had stolen from me, the confidence I never really had.

Finally feeling safe from the monster and having a plan for feeling safe at work, I began to let my guard down. I started to walk around the store during my breaks. I started to take care of myself. I was putting in the effort of rebuilding. My children needed their mother. I felt like I could go somewhere in this company. I wanted to learn every department, become a manager, and eventually do something great. I was sure I could do it. Work was going well. I had learned every single area. I was the person they called when they needed someone to cover any department. I helped train new employees, and I helped set up new stores.

Finally Divorced

On October 26, 2004, I went to court, and I got my divorce. I had to wait for him to file for it, and then I was able to push it through. The previous spring, we had lost our home due to Lissa and unlawful activities she had participated in back when I had originally left with Tony a few years earlier. We moved into a crappy apartment; it was all I could afford. I was living paycheck to paycheck. Every single day was work and kids.

This was the best day of my life. I was free from his abuse. I began walking and eating healthy. The chains were removed, and I had full legal custody of both of my babies. He had no chance of taking my babies as he had promised me. I would still live in fear, but I could start to rebuild. I was going to get things moving into the right direction. After they turned me down on a promotion I was qualified for the third time, I decided I had to do something else, and I went to beauty school.

I was still dancing around my max weight of 412 pounds. I was the only Caucasian woman in the school. I was reminded regularly I was the minority here. I had a lot of talent for hair and makeup. I enjoyed going to school; the harassment was getting to me. I was being bullied and experiencing racism I never had before. This made my school years feel like it was nothing.

My days consisted of waking up really early, dropping my two babies at childcare, and going to beauty school, where I was tortured by my classmates for being different and having natural talent. Then

I would go to the department store and work my ass to the bone for a company that said they promoted from within but didn't do it if you were not hanging out with the supervisors during your off time. I had seen multiple people who were friends off the clock that had no qualifications get the promotions I was qualified to receive just because of their relationship. I was not that kind of person, and I was getting more and more irritated as I kept seeing the cycle continue. When I got home, my parents had already picked up my kids, fed them dinner, and put them to bed. That meant I would bring my dog for a walk, shower, and go to bed myself just to repeat it the next day.

Maybe PCOS

A year after my son was born, I still had not bled once. I was sent by my regular obstetrician to a specialist. She ran a few tests and did a special ultrasound to tell me I had the beginning signs of what appeared to be polycystic ovaries. She said I was fine, that unless I wanted to have another child any time soon, it was nothing I should worry about. The doctor never told me about the other complications that went along with this possible diagnosis. The idea was given, and no treatment or further testing was completed.

Being a Better Momma

I used the next few months to get to know my babies again. I had been working so much to provide for them that our time spent together was minimal. Three and five, they knew who I was, and I showered them with love every chance I had. I felt I was not doing enough. I collected unemployment for months and enjoyed my babies during that time.

I got a job at a clothing store when my unemployment ran out and started working weekends at the campground we lived at over that summer when my parents lost the house. Eventually, I got a third job as a school bus monitor. I thought I never had time to see my kids before; this made it look like I was spending more time than ever with my children. I was doing everything I could to help my father to provide monetary needs for our family. I felt it was my responsibility to reinforce my mother's knowledge as to what the kids needed every day so that they were always safe and taken care of. I refused to allow her to treat my kids the way she had treated me during my childhood.

A Slight Family Gloss

In those few years that went by faster than fast, Sebastian and Lissa caused my father to lose his company completely. Lissa took court-issued papers and threw them directly into the wood furnace, causing my parents to lose their house to the town for unpaid taxes. We lived in a camper for a summer until the church was able to help us find a place to stay.

Stevie was going to auto body school and was finally diagnosed with mental health issues. He was an alcoholic and joined the church, which in turn helped him get back on his feet, and we built our relationship, one we never had as children. As adults, Stevie and I were like twins. We had a bond like none other. Stevie was a recluse and my biggest fan. I wish he was able to be his own advocate; unfortunately, a lot of people don't realize what they need or how to stand up for themselves until it's too late.

Doctors diagnosed Stevie with schizoaffective disorder when he was well into his twenties. and there was no way for him to reverse the damage already caused to his brain by the years of his self-medicating. As long as Stevie was taking his medications, he was stable and able to function mostly well. He wasn't able to hold down a job or live a healthy lifestyle, but Stevie was able to have relationships he never did before his diagnosis.

Stevie turned to AA and became what is called a "big book thumper." Apparently, that means he followed the twelve steps religiously. I remember missionaries coming to the front door, and he would go out and visit with them every week then a few days a week. Slowly, he began to become a better version of himself. Stevie was baptized Mormon; my parents and Sebastian followed soon after.

I attended the services and activities. I gave them at least two years, and I never once felt the same faith in their beliefs as they did. I respectively left as the bishop felt I did not belong attending any longer if I was not going to become a member of the church. This is when I started working as much as possible.

LDS Church

Around the time of having a newborn son, my daughter recovering from her nose being torn off, and my brother beginning to find himself, we all decided to start attending the church in support of his new lifestyle. Every Sunday, the kids put on something cute, and we had our weekly rituals just like when I was a kid.

Even though I did not follow the Christian faith, that did not mean I was going to prevent my children from making up their own minds. I knew how it felt to be held back from learning things and protected in a world filled with all kinds of things. I wanted my children to know how to protect themselves, have faith in themselves, and they needed a higher power. Who was I to decide what that was going to be?

Every week, we sat in the pews. I sang the same gospel songs I had grown up singing in my old stone castle-like church just a few miles down the road. All the songs were the same songs; the main book was the same Holy Bible.

During my time there, I learned that all Christianity is based on the same words. Each branch is just their own interpretation of what they read. No single religion is completely correct or wrong in their beliefs. I was able to support my parents and brothers in joining the church. I did not share in their faith. I respect every one of the people in the LDS community.

I helped with community events and many other things. I was participating in things that you are not supposed to be involved with without being baptized. The church president made a special accommodation for me because I was freshly out of an abusive situation. We never told anyone how bad things had been or how much Tony's name was able to trigger my panic attacks.

When the church board members asked my parents to leave me behind during special "member only" events, they refused, telling them that I was unable to stay home alone. They never went into details. The board members understood my parents needed to protect me, and I was not going anywhere.

As time progressed, my children grew as did my knowledge of the church and every one of their teachings. I sat down with their missionaries, and we discussed me getting baptized. This must have been the second or third time I was approached on the subject. "You already know and understand the teachings. You already come to the church regularly. The new president thinks if you are going to continue to be a part of the church, you need to become an official member."

I looked at these two young men, the same age as me. "I do not want to offend you. I do not share your faith. I have one major issue holding me back from making such a leap."

They shared a glance between each other, sure they had the answer that many pairs of missionaries had tried and failed before them. This was the first pair who actually wanted to know. "Why? What holds you back from joining the church? What keeps you from sharing our faith? You have faith in God."

"Are you absolutely sure you want to know?" I was sure they were able to handle this inquiry. This was the pair of men whom I would give my ultimate question to. These were the men that were going to be able to give me an answer that made sense enough for me to either stay or walk away.

I was finally feeling healed. During the time between joining the church and this conversation, a lot had happened. We had lost my childhood house, lived a summer in a campground, and moved into a crummy apartment with the help of the church. I was walking every single day. I found faith in myself, faith in my inner goddess. My life was beginning to move forward in the right direction. This was the perfect time to have this conversation without the missionaries making me feel that I was a burden to my parents or the church.

Convinced by their answers in how they found their own faith, they decided to go forward with their own baptisms. I gave them my burning question. "If you can give me a realistic answer as to how Virgin Mary was a virgin, I will get baptized."

Both men looked at each other; their faces were puzzled as they had never contemplated the question. This was the same question that had gotten me kicked out of Sunday school when I was a small child. This is the number one question I will always have for anyone following Christian faith. I believe and follow the basic morals. I have a goddess and god. I believe in what they consider the Holy Ghost.

I respect the people who follow the faith, and I do not judge anyone who is able to take that leap. I am happy for them because they are able to look at her and see Jesus as God's child. I look at Mary, and I see a victim. In my eyes, the entire religion is based on a lie. In my own eyes, she was raped in some form and conceived that baby. I say that because I know when I was molested, by the time it had finally stopped, I could have conceived a child myself. Would that have been a child of God? Would that have been a miracle? No, every year we see the celebration of Jesus, and no one thinks about the idea that his mother was likely a victim.

I did not share my thoughts with the men. I kept them to myself, and I am sure this is going to get a huge blow back because I am saying it now.

A while later, I told Noah about my question. He was the only person who said something I can actually understand. "In my eyes, Mary was a virgin. Even if it was just because she had the innocence of a child. She never did anything wrong. She always behaved with the best of intentions. So whatever happened physically to her to create the baby does not matter. In the end, her virgin mind is what matters and gives me faith."

I respect that answer. I wish he was not upset or annoyed when he shared his point of view with me. I was honestly curious as to how someone can have such a blind faith. I do not think Noah knew I was a child of abuse. I do not think my strong feeling toward Mary's virginity was so closely tied to my own.

Finally, I had the answer I needed. Now I ask because I want to see if there is anyone else who has put in the kind of thought needed to really test their beliefs to a point that gives you the strength in your faith to make it unshakable.

Breaking Point

Eventually, the rigid schedule wore me out. I never got to spend time with my children. I had one or two friends max at any time, and they never really knew me. They only knew what I shared with them. They did not know about Lizzie's older brother or how horrible Tony really was. They did not know about my experience in the ICU. None of that mattered because I had to figure out my life.

My weight began to drop. I lost ninety pounds in six months just by eating healthy, walking daily, and drinking water. I kept it off because I never went back to the lifestyle that brought me to that point in my life. I kept working on losing weight, but it was not as rapidly. I lost over 110 pounds on my own and kept it off for over a decade. Many people who knew me during those horrific days do not recognize me now.

When the stress of everything happening finally got to me, I was forced to give everything up all at once. I was about five hundred hours short of finishing beauty school when the racism got to the point that a client came in with bugs crawling in her hair. I was disgusted, and I didn't want to touch it. The client called one of the colored girls over and she said to me, "Oh, that just…it's totally fine. Just relax." I walked over to our instructor, said something, and was told to do it, although there were, in fact, things crawling in this woman's hair. I felt completely appalled. I was not going to touch this woman's hair; it was just too gross. They could say anything they wanted to. Nothing would change my mind. I was out of there.

I was at work that week, and a really nice assistant manager asked me out for drinks. I kindly turned him down. I said something along the lines of I would not be able to bring him home to meet my father. I didn't mean it in a horrible way, but I was hurting after everything I had just been through. I can understand from his point of view, it was likely taken as a racial remark. A few days later, I was released from the department store. I called everyone out on their behavior. I had no problem being bluntly honest with my point of view. The assistant manager who asked me out a few days prior was not part of the group to let me go. I did point out that he did ask me out to dinner, and I turned him down, so the timing was odd.

I began to learn how important eating for fuel is for your physical and mental health. I was taught to eat whatever was on my plate. My father was a meat-and-potatoes man, making most of our meals very unhealthy. When he was around, we usually shared a giant bag of chips and a container of French onion dip. I drank soda constantly because it was available. In the nineties, everyone drank soda by the buckets, unaware of the long-term effects.

We kept unhealthy snacks easy for the taking while I was pregnant. My daughter lived on McDonald's and junk food because I was just too depressed to try harder. My mother being a manager, she brought home a lot of things she did not need to. This left me with very unhealthy habits as I had learned to just stop eating completely as I had done back when I was a preteen and met my friend Celeste.

Now I began learning a whole new lifestyle. I cut down on soda, slowly switching soda for water. I started walking more and more. I found a website that helped remind me to track what I was doing without making changes at first. Then I would slowly make one little change at a time. I would start sacrificing my time for exercise. I hated it to begin with; I felt like I was just wasting my time.

A few weeks passed; the tiny habits turned into a whole new lifestyle. I almost had no recollection of the old me. I was making time to read a book every day, to write in my journal, to spend time with my babies. I was exercising, eating better, and even sleeping a good amount. Life was still just as stressful as it was a month earlier. I still had the same money problems I had before, but I was not feeling as depressed and hopeless.

Something inside me had begun to shift, very slowly at first. I do not know when it started. I had to force myself at first. I had to be willing to take those first small actions. I had to start tracking where I was at the beginning, a week or two from where I was starting. I needed my starting point. I had to be able to measure my success or failure against something. The website I had found began with a starting point.

That first login and setup was probably the hardest because I had to weigh and measure every part of myself. I was humiliated at how large I let myself become. While I was pregnant, the scale at the OB had reached 412 pounds. I knew I was overweight. I looked in the mirror. I saw my size.

When I stepped on my scale, I was 408. I was not my highest. I was still big. My son was a little over a year old. I did my measurements, my neck, arms, chest, waist, hips, and thighs. Everything made me feel horrible. I also knew this was my starting point. I knew that I had to have something to help me measure where I was starting. I could have turned to my newfound best friend, food.

Instead, I pushed myself to keep going. I had a burning desire inside me. I felt the need to feed that fire, the same one I felt that reminded me I was better than the person who was being hurt constantly by the man she thought loved her. That feeling I had when I had a mission I just had to accomplish because something deep to my core wanted it more than anything.

I was carrying around over two hundred pounds of self-hatred, punishment, and depression. I was carrying around the resentment of my childhood, the neglect and abuse I had endured for years without saying a word. I needed to let it all go. I had to continue down this painful path. I had to let myself move forward. No amount of reliving the trauma, the pain, was going to cause me to fall backward. I refused to let anything hold me from being the person I wanted to see myself as when I looked into the mirror.

Right now, looking in the mirror, all I could see was the victim of my life. I needed to be a strong mother. I needed to be healthy in mind, body, and spirit. I knew my faith was in the Goddess. I had let her go a long time ago. I found her again when I looked up at the moon. I felt her deep inside myself, the strength she gave me when I was sure I would fail. I was sure I never would. I kept going as difficult as it got every single time.

Learning to Enjoy Sex

Celeste had this saying she lived by, which most people have heard: "To get over your ex, get under the next." I was traumatized by that. I had a lot of female friends who seemed to live by the same philosophy. I had been single for years by now, and I had a physical desire to get out there and start loving my body. I never had the chance to; I was still really overweight. I had not started losing yet.

I was afraid of men. I could not put myself into a normal situation like my dear friend at the time did, going out and dating like she did, meeting guys at a bar or restaurant. I wanted to meet a man who would understand my terms and treat me the way I wanted and needed at the time, a man who would respect my boundaries and emotional limitations.

I decided to go online and start talking to a few guys. I was okay with online talking. I was able to build my online presence and get to know whom I wanted to be inside. I just had to gain the courage to get this online persona to come out into my real world. I was blogging and talking in chat rooms. Online, I felt like I was my true self. I was open and honest, whereas in the real world, I was living in fear that Tony would come from any dark corner to hurt me again or try to take one of my children.

As I was scrolling one day, I came across a face I knew very well: Josh, my schoolmate's older brother. He had always been a nice guy. I knew his family pretty well, and he was very discreet. We talked about what I wanted and needed from him, how long ago my last relationship was and vague details about the type of man he was.

When people asked me about my children's father, I only would say he was their donor and it was a very abusive relationship. I never got into details. If they pressed, I would say he was abusive mentally, physically, and sexually. That was more than enough for them to realize that this was a subject I was not willing to talk about openly at the time for either their or my own protection.

Now when I talk about that time in my life, I do not go into detail because I do not want to make the other person uncomfortable. At the time, I did not have the emotional strength to deal with the pain Tony caused me.

Josh was respectful and gentle-hearted and understood everything I needed from him. There were days that I needed his physical touch and days where I just needed his friendship. He taught me that a man's touch was not like David or Tony. A man's touch can be something that is affectionate and enjoyable.

This was the first time I was honestly able to enjoy sex. I did not know how much fun and pleasure I could have from the same kind of touch that made my skin grow cold and my mind go numb. Josh taught me in our short time together how wonderful it is to feel physical love. Even though it was not the type of love you share with someone you want to live a life with, this was the type of sex that you want to have; it is the kind that everyone should enjoy with every sexual partner.

Josh was exactly what I needed to help me get over the traumatic pain I had associated with sex. He taught me that I could enjoy it without guilt. He gave me my first pleasurable experience. That was something we aimed to achieve every time we got together, and he taught me how to physically love my body in ways I never had before.

When we set up our arrangements, I was very clear as to what I needed. I was not going to find a father for my children. I was a single mother, and my children were off limits. Josh respected that, and we never had time together when my toddlers were around. This was a time for the two of us to get our physical needs met, and family events were completely off-limits. If either of us began to have emotional ties to the other person and it was not returned, the whole arrangement was off. We would remain friends, and we would not have hard feelings toward each other.

Both of us were in a place in our lives where having a romantic relationship was not an option. We both had a physical desire and wanted to be with someone who would help us to fulfill our needs without having to worry about the commitment of making a future together. We agreed our arrangement would have an expiration date even though it was unsure how long it would last.

As his heart healed from whatever he had to go through, my heart was not at the same place as his. I felt him beginning to get more attached to me and feeling that our relationship was developing into something I was unable to handle emotionally. Our physical relationship started to grow vines into the emotional parts. I felt the need to pull back from him, and Josh respected my choice.

It hurt my heart to break his, but I was not in a place where I could give him the love he deserved. I had to respect our arrangement and back out as the deal had stated. Months later, we tried one more hookup, and we both felt that it was the wrong choice. All of the things that made it great before were gone. We had physically enjoyed it. Everything that made sharing sex together with Josh was no longer part of what we had.

Connecting with the Goddess when I was fourteen made my gut feel like it was on fire. I was starting to feel that again now that I knew how pleasurable sexuality was supposed to be. I started to really focus my energy on everything that brought out those good emotions. I wanted to focus on anything that made the depression fade and bring out only the favorable parts.

I was now exercising every single day because the physical activity made me feel like I had accomplished something good. I may have only walked a mile with my dog. It took me over an hour at first as I was winded and I had to push myself. Over time, the same mile took me under twenty minutes, and my dog loved every single one of our walks. I began bringing him in the morning before work and at the end of the day before we called it a night.

I was eating better because I learned to fuel my body in a way that made me have energy to think better and focus. When I ate vegetables and whole foods, I discovered I was able to focus on my children better. My attitude was happier. I had more patience for them when they were having normal toddler tantrums. I noticed if I ate something that was processed, I would become irritable and cranky. The children deserved a mother who was not angry like the mother I had growing up.

I was reading more and more books, focusing on my mind. I needed to read. My brain was a sponge for knowledge. I read books by Amanda Quick for pleasurable distraction. I read self-help books for self-development, and I read spiritual books for obvious reasons. I researched a lot of different religious beliefs at this time. I wanted to make sure I was confident in my decision and dedication to my Goddess.

I always believed in Mother Earth. I have yet to meet a single person who does not believe she is the creator of all things. I have learned one of her names is "Gaia." As a result, I can say without hesitation my Goddess is Gaia. I feel that every person has an equal counterpart, and they may change over time. I was unable to name whom her partner was, and I did not care. I needed to focus on Gaia and everything she could bring me.

Many people turn to Christianity or another faith. This was my faith. I turned to Gaia. I studied religions from all over the world before I fully committed to what my gut had said my entire life. I just wanted to be sure I was not making a choice I would end up changing later in my lifetime like my own parents had done.

After really embracing my beliefs and accepting the word "witch" as what I choose it to mean, I had found my own power.

In my life, "witch" is a word of power. The victims of the Salem Witch Trials were people who were seen as threats to their community. Those are the people who may have been able to make major changes in the world if they were left alone to do whatever they were destined to do. As a result of their deaths, our world has been changed. Many other events have occurred. We have since learned to obtain our own power and concentrate it in a way that will make changes to the world we live in.

Facing Trauma

During my healing process, one of the biggest challenges I faced was learning how to overcome my traumas. This is when I experimented with different types of treatments. There really is no one solution for any single person and what worked for me may not necessarily work for you. I chose to go through a list of treatments and see what worked best for me. The funny part is that the first time I tried something, it may not have helped. When I gave it a chance again later on, it unlocked a piece of my mind that I had forgotten about.

- Talk therapy
- Yoga
- Exercise
- Brain stimulation therapy
- Antidepressants
- Acupuncture
- Journaling
- Guided meditation
- Reading countless self-help books
- Spending time with friends
- Exposure therapy

Some of my coping mechanisms had to be developed over time. I could no longer use food as a crutch for fear of putting all the weight back on. I had witnessed my mother and Stevie losing and regaining weight multiple times over the years because they never faced whatever caused them to gain their weight in the beginning.

I also tried some unhealthy ways to cope with my emotions. I chose to keep these off the list because no one needs to try the options that can and will ruin lives by following a path of self-destruction.

I was one major step ahead of my family. I knew that I had put on my weight as armor to shield myself from the pain I was suffering. I was using food to numb myself whenever I did not want to face the reality of the situation. I literally was stuffing my feelings by stuffing my face, and I used my pregnancy as my excuse to not feel guilty. I did not care about the additional weight or how hard it would be to lose it later. I only cared about feeling numbness.

From my understanding, that is the reason addicts choose to fall back on their self-destructive tendencies. They choose to drink or get high because they feel it is easier to numb their emotional pain than to deal with it. I have had to learn the hard way pushing off facing your emotions rather than just dealing with them makes the problem worse overall.

If I had screamed that night, someone would have come running in. They would have seen my naked, bruised, and bloodied body. They also would have made sure I had no chance of hiding what that man had done. Tony would likely be in jail or dead. I did not scream. I made a choice, and I was frozen in fear that night. I do not blame myself for being a victim. I felt I had to save my family from the trauma that I was experiencing. Why did any of them need to suffer the way I had been for so long? I was used to protecting others; I had done it my entire life up to that point.

During my healing process, I chose that it was now my turn to protect myself as well as the people I cared for, my children. I was already taking care of the two of them. I was slowly learning how to take care of myself. I was gaining confidence with each day and each step of my progress.

I saw my grandmother after my first initial weight loss, and I was thrilled with her response to see my success. She was proud of my changes. I chose to stop being a victim; not everyone can make that decision. I kept pushing myself because I wanted to make her proud. I never made anyone feel proud of me, and this was a new feeling.

Once I started to find an emotion I enjoyed, I would do everything I could to continue to have that feeling. I was so used to feeling numb that anything that brought me positivity was completely new. I had to learn to enjoy that sensation. I would do almost anything to keep repeating this experience.

Loving My Life as a Single
Divorced Mother of Two

____

I was at a point in my life I had accepted my life as it was. I was happy to be single, and I enjoyed putting my children first. I made time for myself, my health, and my heart. I had a man whom I could call when I needed someone physically. When that relationship expired, I did not mind. I had enough other things going on in my life. I did not care if I was going to meet someone again or not.

I was not going to date; I did not want or need a relationship. I was working a lot, providing my children with everything they needed. I was finding a balance in my life and happy with my choice of staying single. I was finally happy. I truly loved myself.

Falling Fast

In a strange fate of events, I found myself at a county fair with my kids for the first time in our lives. A week earlier, a freak accident caused a tragedy resulting in my now four-year-old son having a broken femur. Luckily, everyone involved that day was all right in the end, and we were able to make the most out of the experience.

This led to me having my first day off from three jobs coinciding together with the same day that my dear friend had off, and she always went to this particular fair. I decided to pack up my children, the temporary handicap flag, the wheelchair, and head out to meet her there to spend the day walking around the fairgrounds for the first time.

I really just needed something to do with my children that did not include sitting at home being sad with my son stuck in his chair and having nothing to do. My daughter was restless as any six-year-old would be after spending so much time waiting on her little brother hand and foot because he was a nosy little brother who was in the wrong place at the wrong time and ended up paying for it. My son almost paid for his curiosity with his life, and my daughter was not the kind of sister to let him forget it. She was the kind that would make sure he was well taken care of while also making sure he remembered why his leg was broken.

At the fair, we met my friend's cousin, the same man she had been trying to set me up to go out with for months and possibly years earlier. I remember seeing him, and the first thought in my mind after noting how short he was in comparison to most of the other people around was how much larger his biceps were than everyone else's. "I wonder what it would be like to have those wrapped around me," was my immediate thought.

During the week before the tragic event, I had been talking to a friend's brother about possibly meeting in a few weeks. I was just about to repeat the arrangement that I had with Josh, but this would have been different than that because I was not the same person anymore. I had lost over a hundred pounds since the situationship with Josh. I had learned to love myself, and I was open to whatever possibilities life had in store for me now.

This man and I spent the day with my friend and my children walking around the fairgrounds talking and hanging out. We did not do anything special or out of the ordinary. It was just a nice day of visiting and getting to know each other while looking at all the events and different things happening.

When it was time to go, I hesitantly asked him if he wanted my number. I was still very shy and nervous. I did not know he was just as nervous as I was. I made the first move, only because I asked my friend if he was interested and if I should. I gave him my number, and we went our separate ways.

The next day was Monday; I had sun poisoning. My skin was red with water-filled bubbles, and I had a fever. I was ill, and I should have gone to the emergency room. Instead, I went to work, got home, drank a ton of water, and was miserable. I repeated the process Tuesday. On Wednesday, I was finally feeling better.

On Wednesday night, I got home late to a message from my father that a "black-sounding man called me." My father was just like that. He did not mean to be; it was his personality. He was just as blunt as I was, and there was no filter to his thoughts. I guess there's no real filter to mine either come to think of it. I called him back, and we talked for a while.

Then we talked again on Thursday, making plans to go out on our first date the following night. We had just met that Sunday. We had no idea where things were going to go or how things might end up. We made it a habit to talk to each other every day at a minimum.

A few weeks later, someone mentioned to me it sounded like he was my boyfriend. I was starting to seem happy for the first time. My children were seeing me more often, and every day, the sun seemed to shine a little brighter. We talked about the labels of calling each other a couple and if we were comfortable with that or not, what it meant, and if we wanted to explore where things would be going. We agreed we would ride the waves of our relationship and see where we ended up.

Just under three months later, it was our first Christmas together, and I had just met his mother. She gave me a little box, and my entire body froze. Could he have been giving me an engagement ring like my father did to my mother on their first Christmas? He didn't know the story—that didn't make sense! I opened the little jewelry box, and a full body wave of relief took over me as I realized it was a rose quartz teardrop pendant necklace. I was the first person his mother shared any of her late mother's jewelry with. She never even gave a piece to one of her two sisters at this point. I was definitely special to him.

A year later, we moved into our first apartment together. My children had been calling him "Dad" for a long time by now. We had decided that we wanted to see if we would make a good couple full-time. We had been spending almost every single day together leading up to moving in together, and it was the next logical step.

By the writing of this book, we've been together for sixteen years. There's been highs and lows. I have not regretted any one of the choices I have made with him. I love the life we have built together, and we are raising our family.

Letting Go

People take an entire lifetime to get where I have now been able to get. I let go of my anger toward all the people who had hurt me. I put myself in each of their mental situations and thought about how difficult I found it for me to let go of my own pain and move forward. I was tired of being angry. I had to forgive them so I could move on. I chose to live my life in love.

Those predators did not have someone to love them. I was never going to love them, and they surely did not love me. They also did not deserve to have any more power over my life. They had stolen too much of my life already. I was now choosing to live my life surrounded by love because my children needed to know what love is.

I felt love the first time I met my daughter. I felt courage the first time when I found out I was pregnant with my son. I was going to feed those two emotions and make sure they did not have to learn the horrible things I had endured most of my life. I had chosen to turn a page and let go of the anger. I let go of the pain connected to every piece of the abuse done to me.

I began to ask my mother questions about her childhood, what her parents were like when she was a kid. I wanted to know what made her be the kind of parent she was. I learned so much about her with the answers she did not give me, more than from the things she did say.

Stevie and I started to open up about how we felt growing up. We talked about the fights and how much I feared him every single day. He did not remember most of the explosions he had released on me. As an adult, he was diagnosed with bipolar disorder. This meant most of those attacks came during a manic episode. Nothing I did or did not do could have triggered his response. He was on medication. We built a trust we never had as children.

Stevie had confided in me the abuse he endured during the time our parents were unavailable to us. We assumed our oldest brother was also a victim, but I never told Stevie what Sebastian had done to cause my relationship to completely dissolve. I was never going to tell anyone. Even through this tell-all story, I almost feel badly for painting him in such a bad light.

Each of us children had our own type of traumatic experience. Our parents did the best they could at the time. They failed us in ways they may never truly know. I hope for their sakes, I was able to protect them from knowing the extent of the pain I survived. My mother passed away before I started writing this. I had tried many times to get the words out. I have had the notes compiled for decades, waiting to be put together.

After my mother passed, I felt a weight lift from me. Everything I was trying to protect was gone. I no longer had to worry about letting my mother know how much I felt she had let me down. She blamed me for our house burning down when I was just under three years old. I clung to her leg in fear and refused to leave her side.

From her point of view, she was unable to get to the fire extinguisher on the other side of the house. From my point of view, I was a baby, just out of diapers. I was scared, and I needed the arms of my mother to keep me safe. Looking back, I am sure I saved her life by clinging to her like I did. The universe took away our physical house but saved our lives.

That was the first time I protected someone with my life. I believe it was the reason I spent the rest of my life protecting other people, even the people who never deserved my protection. I have protected people when they hurt me, when they were doing things they should not have been doing and when they were a villain in my story. I protected my friend from her brother by becoming a victim because I did not know how to tell an adult what was happening.

I protected my brother when he was hurting me because he was mentally ill, and I was getting blamed for his behavior. I protected my first boyfriend, who later became my first husband, because I thought that is what you're supposed to do when you love someone. I protected my second husband from his own behaviors that later came back around.

I did all that with the best of intentions. I had to learn to forgive myself for being a victim, for putting myself in a situation where I allowed myself to be hurt, used, or abused for whatever reasons. I was afraid to stand up for myself for a long time. I was afraid that people would judge me for failing to be something that I never really was.

One day, I realized that I am a great mother. I am a great person. I am a friend. I live my life pure of heart and full of love. I do not want to cause harm to my abusers. I want to see the people who hurt me get the help they so desperately need so they may become better people and change the world for the good.

I want to see all the victims in the world let go of their own pain and find their own self-worth. You did not deserve to be treated the way you had been treated in the past. Your monster chose to hurt you because you were convenient. There is no better reason than that alone.

Forgive yourself because that is the absolute first step in overcoming all traumas in your lifetime and moving forward to something wonderful and great.

Once I stopped blaming myself for everything horrible that happened in my life and realized how all the things that were done to me had happened because of a disgusting chain of events, I realized that I had the power to live my best life. I hold the power to be my own hero.

If I can be my own hero and I can change my life for the better, then so can you. My children and their friends have come to me when their lives have needed someone to help them. I am the guiding light in tragedy. I am a beacon of hope during a storm. I have been through the worst things in life, and I have made it through.

Every single person in the world has that kind of ability.

About the Author

———————————

Maryellen grew up in a small rural community with emotionally unavailable parents. As the youngest of three children and the only female, she was treated differently than her brothers. After a childhood of abuse and neglect, she fought through the adolescence of her life trying to figure out what path to take. Her journey was one she could never have anticipated.

As Maryellen realized that she was going to have to stand up for herself and her children, she decided that she had to become her own hero and do everything she could to move forward in a positive light.

Now she lives just twenty miles from her childhood home with her own family, teaching them everything she had to learn on her own and sharing her story and sparkle every chance she gets.